Test Your English Vocabulary in

Elementary **Use**

Michael McCarthy
Felicity O'Dell

CAMBRIDGE UNIVERSITY PRESS
Cambrudge, New York, Melbourne, Madrid, Cape Town, Singapore, São Paulo

Cambridge University Press
The Edinburgh Building, Cambridge CB2 2RU, UK

www.cambridge.org
Information on this title: www.cambridge.org/9780521534062

First published 2004
3rd printing 2005

Printed in the United Kingdom at the University Press, Cambridge

A catalogue record for this publication is available from the British Library

ISBN-13 978-0-521-53406-2 paperback
ISBN-10 0-521-53406-2 paperback

Contents

Introduction

Who is this book for?

Test Your English Vocabulary in Use (Elementary) aims to help students check their vocabulary learning. It can be used by all elementary learners of English who want to test their vocabulary. It will also be useful for learners who are using *English Vocabulary in Use (Elementary)* and want to test their progress. Learners can use this test book alone, but the tests can also be used by a teacher working with groups of students.

How is the book organised?

The tests correspond in focus to the 60 units of *English Vocabulary in Use (Elementary)*. The Contents page shows you how the tests are grouped by category. Every test is independent and you do not need to do the tests in a particular order, as they do not become progressively more difficult.

Each test has a total of 30 marks, and the number of marks for the exercises is given within each test. There is an Answer key at the back of the book. A list of phonemic symbols is given on page 91.

Also at the back of the book, you will find a Personal diary. Here, you can make a note of the words you found difficult to remember.

How do I use this book?

If you are working alone with this book, first look at the Contents page, and choose the tests that interest you. You will find different types of vocabulary tests, such as tests on everyday verbs, tests on words and grammar, tests on different topic areas. Try to do different kinds of tests to give you variety. Remember, you do not need to do the tests in a particular order.

If you are using *English Vocabulary in Use (Elementary)*, you can use the tests after finishing a unit from the book. You can do this immediately after finishing a unit, or wait a while (e.g. a week) and use the test as a revision exercise.

You can use the tests more than once by writing the answers in pencil and rubbing them out when you have checked your answers. Alternatively, you could write your answers on a separate sheet of paper.

When you have checked your answers, you could write any words you had problems with in your Personal diary.

The marking scheme

You will find notes on the marking scheme at the beginning of the Answer key on page 64. The marking scheme is just to give you an idea of how well you know the vocabulary, but you do not have to use this marking scheme if you do not want to.

Talking about language

1.1

10 marks

Complete the table with the correct grammar word from the list.

preposition   phrase   noun   paragraph   adjective   plural
adverb   sentence   dialogue   ~~verb~~   singular

	Grammar word	Meaning	Example
	verb	something we do	go, eat, look
1		a piece of text (one or more sentences) beginning on a new line	This test is about words for talking about language. You can score 30 points.
2		a word that describes a verb	quickly, happily
3		a conversation between two people	TOM: Where's my pen? NORA: On the table.
4		just one	car, student, girl
5		a person or thing	teacher, cat, chair
6		a word that describes a person or thing	big, good, tall
7		a complete idea in writing; it starts with a capital letter and ends in a full stop (.)	Yesterday I went to the beach with a friend.
8		a little word used before a noun	at, on, from
9		a group of words	in my room, a new car
10		more than one	cars, students, girls

1.2

10 marks

Fill the gaps with words which tell you how to do the exercises in this book.

1 C.................. the mistakes in these sentences.
2 Fill the g.................. in the sentences.
3 M.................. the words on the left with the words on the right.
4 A.................. another example to this list of drinks.
5 C.................. this sentence with information about yourself.

1.3

5 marks

Answer the questions.

1 What is the plural of *boy*: boys or boy's?
2 Is *nice* an adjective or an adverb?
3 Which word is the verb in this sentence? My sister works in Hong Kong.
4 What is the singular of *men*?
5 Which of these words is a noun: sing, out, long, door?

1.4

5 marks

Match the instructions on the left with the exercises on the right.

Instructions
1 Fill the gap.
2 Correct the mistake.
3 Add an example.
4 Answer the question.

5 Complete the sentence.
6 Complete the dialogue.

Exercises
a blue, yellow, green
b It was her birthday so I gave her a present.
c It's very easy to make mistakes with prepositions.
d MONA: It's cold today.
   DAVID: Yes, I think it's going to snow.
e She came at the morning. She came in the morning.
f What is your phone number? It's 378654.

Your score

/30

2.1
10 marks

Which words go together? Circle the correct underlined answer.

Example: go in/by/on train

1 bad at/in/on maths
2 go with/by/on foot
3 a high/tall man
4 make/do an exercise
5 make/do a mistake

6 do/have a party
7 have/make a shower
8 happy/sunny weather
9 pretty girl/day/car
10 drive/ride/go a car

2.2
10 marks

Put the words in the box into four word families. Then give each word family a name.

bike	mother	car	train	juice	daughter
bus	tea	green	blue	red	milk
father	~~black~~	motorbike	coffee	brother	son

Colours			
black			

2.3
10 marks

Match each word with the picture that can help you to learn it.

Example: door ..9..

a

b

c

d

e

f

g

h

i

j

k

1 up   ....
2 down   ....
3 hat   ....
4 cloud   ....
5 car   ....
6 foot   ....
7 happy   ....
8 sad   ....
9 knife   ....
10 glass   ....

3 Have/had/had

3.1
5 marks

What are these people doing? Write sentences using *have*.

Example: He's having a swim.

1 ....

2 ....

3 ....

4 ....

5 ....

3.2
5 marks

Match the phrases using *have* on the left with the explanations on the right.

1 have an appointment   a enjoy something
2 have a go   b be free to do something
3 have a good time   c try something
4 have a word with someone   d must be somewhere at a fixed time
5 have the time to do something   e speak to someone

3.3
10 marks

Fill the gaps with the correct form of *have, have to* or *have got*.

1 I asked for stamps in the shop but they .... any so I .... go to the post office.
2 I .... a headache yesterday so I didn't go to class.
3 .... you .... a dictionary? Can I .... a look at it please?
4 Everyone .... pay for the school trip seven days before we leave. That means we .... just three days before we .... pay.
5 Do you .... a moment? I'd like to ask you a question.
6 I .... my hair cut yesterday. Do you like it?

3.4
5 marks

What can you say using *have*? Fill the gaps.

1 *(Someone is leaving for the airport to fly to New York.)* Bye-bye! .... !
2 *(Someone shows you a new mobile phone with computer games on it.)* Wow! Can I .... ?
3 *(Someone says they have just got their holiday photographs from the photo shop.)* Can I .... ?
4 *(Someone is going out for the evening to a restaurant, then to a party.)* Bye! .... !
5 *(You want to speak to someone about something important.)* Can .... ?

3.5
5 marks

Fill the gaps.

1 We had a .... in the new Chinese restaurant yesterday.
2 I have a .... with the boss at 10.30, but I can see you at 11 o'clock.
3 She has an .... at the doctor's at 5pm today.
4 In our English classes, we have .... every day after the lesson and we have an .... at the end of every term.

Your score
/30

Go/went/gone

4.1

10 marks

Fill the gaps with the right word.

Example: Let's go ....*to*........ the cinema this evening.

1 My mother goes to work .... train.
2 The old lady went .... the house and .... the street.
3 My husband went .... on business last week.
4 Oliver went .... the stairs to his bedroom on the top floor.
5 In the morning I go .... to my office in the lift but at the end of the day I go .... the stairs.
6 I like to go to work .... foot.
7 We've had a lovely holiday but we have to go .... home tomorrow.
8 Is this bus going .... the railway station?

4.2

5 marks

Which meaning of *go* is used in each sentence? Write a, b or c by each sentence.

a move from one place to another   b do an activity   c talk about plans for the future

Example: I go to work by bike.   *a*

1 Are you going to watch the football match tonight?
2 Larry goes to Paris on business every year.
3 I love going sightseeing when I'm on holiday.
4 What are you going to do next year?
5 Do you like going shopping?

4.3

5 marks

Which activity is each person doing? Use an expression with *going*.

Example: Dan is going skiing.

Dan

1 Nora

2 Harry

3 Mel and Bob

4 Terry and Sarah

5 Nick

4.4

10 marks

Look at Jim's diary. What is he going to do each day? Write ten sentences.

Example:

On Monday Jim is going to have lunch with Mary.

MONDAY
Have lunch with Mary.
Evening-meet Tom and Ricky.

TUESDAY
Visit grandmother.

WEDNESDAY
Meet Pat for dinner.

THURSDAY
Morning-have my hair cut.
Evening- play table tennis with Mary.

FRIDAY
Write report for work.
Phone Aunt Sally.

SATURDAY
Buy Tom's birthday present.

SUNDAY
Give Tom his present.
Take Mary to Tom's party.

NOTES

5 Do/did/done

5.1
10 marks

Fill the gaps with the correct form: *do/does*, *did* or *done*. Two of the forms you need are negative.

1 MOTHER: Have you .... your homework?
   TOM: Yes, I .... it last night.
2 GERRY: .... your brother live at home with your parents?
   LIAM: No, he .... , but my sister ....
3 PAUL: .... you like the concert yesterday?
   ULLA: Yes, I .... Why .... you go?
   PAUL: Oh, I had to study for my exam.
4 RITA: I feel really tired.
   DON: So .... I.
   RITA: We've .... a lot of work today.

5.2
5 marks

Write each sentence in another way, using *do*.

Sentence	Same sentence using do
Example: She's working in the garden.	She's doing the gardening.
1 What is your job?	
2 How do you spend the weekends?	
3 Let me wash the dishes.	
4 I always clean my house on Saturdays.	
5 I worked very hard but I failed the exam.	

5.3
15 marks

Correct the mistakes in these sentences.

1 MICHAEL: What does your father?
   JANE: He's a lorry-driver. (*1 mistake*)
2 I don't like do homework but I know I have to do.
   (*2 mistakes*)
3 He do a lot of business with companies in the USA
   nowadays. (*1 mistake*)
4 I saw her at the gym. She was done some exercises
   that looked very hard. (*1 mistake*)
5 DIANA: Liz, what you are doing with all those clothes?
   LIZ: I do my washing. All my clothes are dirty.
   (*2 mistakes*)
6 FATHER: Ivan, to do your homework now!
   IVAN: No. Not now. I do it later. Please Dad!
   FATHER: No! I want you do it now! (*3 mistakes*)
7 MARIA: I does my best to learn all the new words every day.
   ANONA: So does I, but then I forget them again. (*2 mistakes*)

Your score
/30

8 In our family, my father do the washing-up every day, my mother
   is do the gardening, but my brother never doing anything! (*3 mistakes*)

6 Make/made/made

6.1 What is each person making? Write sentences.

Ivan   *Example:* Ivan is making a noise.

1 Pam ....   6 Phil ....

2 Tim ....   7 Sophie ....

3 Rose ....   8 Vincent ....

4 Chris ....   9 Katy ....

5 Isabelle ....   10 Nathan ....

6.2 Put these words in the right column.

lunch	your homework	a noise	an appointment
a mistake	some exercises	the housework	your best
the dishes	a decision	the cooking	

Do	Make
	lunch

6.3 There are six mistakes in this letter. Correct them – the first one is done for you.

Dear Jane,

                                      did

I've had such a busy day. After school I made my homework. I did it very quickly so I think I probably did a lot of mistakes. Then my friend and I went to a film. The hero died so it made us feel very happy. After the film we went to a café. The food smelt very good, which made me feel very thirsty. The food wasn't very good, but at least I didn't have to make the dishes.

I've got to make an exam next week, but let's meet at the weekend.

Love,

Annie

7 Come/came/come

7.1 What are the people saying? Fill the gaps using expressions with *come*.

5 marks

1  Hi Mum! I've finished my shopping and I'm ....
See you in 20 minutes.

2  Timmy, ... ! Don't stand there!

3  Hi, Jane. I'm just .... the station. My train was late.

4 His name's Miguel and I think he .... Mexico.

5 'I'm sorry, Madam, your jacket will not be ready till tomorrow.'  Oh. Okay. I .... tomorrow.

7.2 Match the underlined words on the left with the definitions on the right.

5 marks

1 Jo is in hospital. Do you want to come and see
her with me?
2 We're going to the park. Do you want to come along?
3 I came across an old photo of you yesterday.
4 Come round at about five o'clock and have a cup of tea.
5 Her name came up in conversation.

a found by chance
b go to someone's house
c visit a person or place
d was mentioned
e go with someone to a place

7.3 Correct the mistakes in these conversations.

20 marks

1 LORNA: Has your brother come back of Germany yet?
   JAMES: Yes, he came to home last Friday. (*2 mistakes*)
2 HILDA: Do you know Stockholm? I've never been there.
   RYAN: Yes, I came there last summer for a few days. (*1 mistake*)
3 STEVE: What nationality is Tanya? Where she comes from?
   FELIX: She's coming from Moscow. She's Russian. (*2 mistakes*)
4 ANNA: I was surprised to see Julia in your office.
   NANCY: Yes, she didn't even knock. She just came into. (*1 mistake*)
5 EVA: Do you know what the English word 'cabbage' means?
   PACO: Yes, it came upon in the lesson yesterday. It's a vegetable. (*1 mistake*)
6 ADA: Would you like to coming round to my house this evening to watch a video?
   NIK: Yes, but my cousin is staying with me. Can he come long?
   ADA: Of course. He can came too. (*3 mistakes*)

8 Take/took/taken

8.1 How long did it take people to do these things? Make sentences using *took*.

10 marks

Sam *Example:*	8.00 – left home to go to work It took Sam half an hour to go/get to work.	8.30 – arrived at work
1 Miranda	7.30 – left home to go to work	8.30 – arrived at work
2 Tony	9.00 – started checking e-mails	9.20 – finished checking e-mails
3 Maggie	19.00 – started doing homework	20.15 – finished doing homework
4 Jeremy	10.00 – got on plane to fly to Paris	11.30 – arrived in Paris
5 Julia	12.45 – started eating lunch	12.55 – finished eating lunch
6 Mark	15.15 – started writing report	17.45 – finished writing report
7 Angela	18.25 – got on train to go to London	22.05 – arrived in London
8 Paul	10.00 – started repairing bike	13.30 – finished repairing bike
9 Rosemary	July 1 – started writing story	Sept 30 – finished writing story
10 Ken	December 1995 – started writing poem	December 2002 – finished writing poem

8.2 Use the words below to write full sentences.

10 marks

Example: I / take / French course / last year.
            I took a French course last year.

1 I / take / train / when / go / airport / last summer
2 Anita / take / English exam / tomorrow
3 Kay / want / take / Greek lessons
4 Her father / take / bus / the office
5 Pete / take / driving test / yesterday

8.3 Look at the pictures and write the English words beside them. Then choose the right word to fill each gap.

10 marks

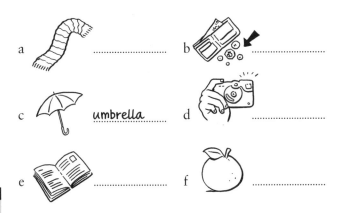

a ....

b ....

c umbrella

d ....

e ....

f ....

Example: It's raining – take your
           umbrella with you.

1 You'll have time to read on the train, so don't forget to take a
  ....
2 You'll want something to eat, so take an .... with you.
3 You might want to take some photos, so do take your ....
4 Take some .... – you may want to buy some postcards.
5 It'll be cold in the evening – take a .... with you.

Your score
/30

9.1

10 marks

Fill the gaps with the correct form of *take* or *bring*.

1 She often comes to see me and always .... me chocolates.
2 I'm just .... this book back to the library. I'll be back in half an hour.
3 She borrowed my camera but she .... it back the next day.
4 Are you going to the kitchen? Will you .... me a glass of water?
5 .... this letter to the post office and post it for me, will you?

9.2

10 marks

What could you say? Use *take* or *bring* in your answer. There may be more than one possible answer.

1 Your friend has to catch a train. You have a car. Offer to drive them to the station.
2 A friend is going into town. You have a parcel which you want to post.
3 You're having a party at your house. One of your friends plays the guitar. Invite them with their guitar.
4 You've just bought a sweater but the size is wrong. Tell a friend what you're going to do when you go to town tomorrow.
5 A good friend is going to Belgium for a few days. You'd like some Belgian chocolates.

9.3

10 marks

Correct the mistakes in these e-mails.

Tuesday 4 March 2003

Hi Ellen,

Guess what? Tim takes me to the cinema last night and today when I was studying at home he came to see me and is taking me some flowers! I think he must be in love with me!

Bye,
Marian

Wednesday 5 March 2003

Dear Marian,

Yes, I think Tim is in love with you! Why don't you brought him to our party on Friday so we can all meet him? Oh, and take that new CD you told me about, I'd like to hear it.

Love,
Ellen

Thursday 6 March 2003

Hi again Ellen,

Thanks for inviting Tim. He said yes.
I'll bring the CD to the party tomorrow and I'll leave it with you.
You can took it back when you come to see me on Sunday.

Take care,
Marian.

Your score

/30

Get/got/got

10.1

10 marks

Fill the gaps in 1–5 with an adjective (e.g. *dark*, *hot*, etc.). Fill the gaps in 6–10 with a noun (e.g. *stamps*, *doctor*, etc.).

Example: If you are ill, you want to get ..well/better.. .

1 If you are cold, you want to get ....
2 If your life is boring, you want it to get more ....
3 If your working day is very long, you'd like it to get ....
4 If you are poor, you'd probably like to get ....
5 If someone is fat and they eat less and do a lot of exercise they will probably get ....

Example: If you are hungry, you want to get some ..food.......... .

6 Before you go on a train journey, you have to get a ....
7 You go to the bank or a cash machine when you want to get some ....
8 You go to the baker's when you want to get some ....
9 When it's your birthday you probably get some ....
10 You check your e-mail program to see if you have got any new ....

10.2

10 marks

Write questions asking how to get to these places.

Example:

How do I get to the airport?

1 ....

2 ....

3 ....

4 ....

5 ....

10.3

10 marks

Fill the gaps with the correct form of *get*.

Example: Dick is planning to go to university ....to get.... a degree in medicine.

1 It's raining and the people at the bus stop .... wet.
2 David and Hilary .... married last July.
3 I'm very thirsty. Could we .... a cup of tea somewhere soon?
4 My dad usually .... home from work at 6.30.
5 My grandfather was ill last week but he .... better now.
6 I'd like .... a job with a big international company.
7 What time do you normally .... to school?
8 My brother .... back from the United States yesterday.
9 I'm going to the shop .... a newspaper.
10 I love sending and .... e-mails.

Your score

/30

11 Phrasal verbs

11.1
10 marks

Fill the gaps in these magazine horoscopes.

Pisces

You and your boss are getting
(1)................ very well these days and this
week she will give you the chance of a
much better job. Say yes immediately;
don't (2)................ it down. If you stay in
the job for another two or three years,
you will have a very interesting career.

Gemini

You have not been well lately, but
you're getting (5)................ it and you will
soon be feeling fine again. But you must
learn to relax. Every evening, (6)................
on the TV, lie on the sofa, (7)................ off
your shoes and forget your problems
for an hour. It's good for you!

Capricorn

It's time to start a new life! Start getting
(3)................ early in the mornings, don't
stay in bed. And now is the time to
(4)................ up your home. Paint the
walls in bright colours, mend those old
windows, buy some new furniture.

Virgo

You spend too much time watching TV.
Even if the weather is horrible, turn
the TV (8)................ , (9)................ your
coat on and go out for a walk. Come
(10)................ ! Start living!

11.2
10 marks

Match the sentences on the left with the sentences on the right.

1 A bomb exploded at the military base today.
2 Her jacket was open and she felt cold.
3 The plane was delayed.
4 She couldn't hear the radio.
5 She decided it was time to go to sleep.

a She turned it up.
b She turned the light off.
c She did it up.
d It went off at 4.45 pm.
e It took off at 4.45 pm.

11.3
10 marks

Correct the mistakes.

1 My teacher is very nice and all the students get in very well with him.
2 I went over working until after midnight because I had an exam the next day.
3 It's raining; put over your raincoat.
4 They offered her the job but she turned it off.
5 I had a bad cold last week but I've got above it now and I feel much better.

Your score
/30

12.1

5 marks

Andy does these things every morning. At what time does he do each thing?

gets up	goes to work	goes to the bathroom	has breakfast	gets to the office	~~wakes up~~

Example: 7.00   <u>wakes up</u>

1 7.05 ....   2 7.10 ....   3 7.30 ....   4 7.45 ....   5 8.30 ....

12.2

5 marks

Andy does these things every evening. At what time does he do each thing?

~~leaves the office~~	has dinner	cleans his teeth	goes to bed	comes home	makes dinner

Example: 5.00   <u>leaves the office</u>

1 5.30 ....   2 6.30 ....   3 7.00 ....   4 10.30 ....   5 11.00 ....

12.3

10 marks

Here are pictures of Andy. What is he doing in each picture? Write sentences.

Example:  <u>Andy is leaving the office.</u>

1 ....

2 ....

3 ....

4 ....

5 ....

6 ....

7 ....

8 ....

9 ....

10 ....

12.4

10 marks

Write questions for these answers. Use either *What time ...?* or *How often ...?*

Example: Q: <u>How often do you listen to the radio?</u>
             A: I listen to the radio every evening.

1 Q: ....
   A: I go to work at 8.15.
2 Q: ....
   A: I clean the house every Saturday.
3 Q: ....
   A: I normally get up at 7 o'clock.
4 Q: ....
   A: I go for a walk every evening.
5 Q: ....
   A: I wash my clothes every week.

6 Q: ....
   A: I usually go to bed at 11.30.
7 Q: ....
   A: I go to the supermarket once a week.
8 Q: ....
   A: I usually come home at 6.30.
9 Q: ....
   A: I go to my friend's house every Friday evening.
10 Q: ....
   A: I write letters every Sunday.

13 Talking

13.1
5 marks

Match the sentence beginnings on the left with the correct endings on the right.

1	I said	a	me her name.
2	She told	b	'I'm hungry.'
3	I told her	c	goodbye.
4	She said	d	the way to the station.
5	We said	e	that she was tired.

13.2
5 marks

Fill the gaps with the correct form of *say* or *tell*.

1   LARRY: Did she .... what time she was arriving?
         RUBY: Yes, her train arrives at 6.30.

2   MICK: Have you .... Jim about the party?
         FRAN: Yes, I've invited him.

3   YOLANDA: Did she .... thanks when you found her credit card?
         PAULA: No, she just took it. You know what she's like.

4   EILEEN: Did Bob .... any jokes at the dinner yesterday?
         KIM: Yes, as usual he had some very funny ones.

5   TOURIST: Can you .... me where the art museum is, please?
   LOCAL PERSON: Yes, just two blocks away from here, on your left.

13.3
10 marks

What do you do in these situations? Use the verb *ask* in your answer.

Example: You are in a new city and want to know what to see, where to eat, etc.
Ask for information (e.g. at the tourist office).

1 You do not know how to get from place A to place B.
2 You are in the street and you don't have your watch on.
3 You are in class and you do not understand a new word.
4 You have finished your meal in a restaurant.
5 Someone is playing a CD very loudly and you are trying to study.

13.4
10 marks

Correct the mistakes in these sentences.

1 The phone's ringing! Will you reply to it, please, David?
2 My best friend lived in Denmark for five years so she talks excellent Danish.
3 I sent him a fax, but he hasn't said back yet.
4 SVEN: How is said 'Milan' in Italian?
   LENA: It's 'Milano'.
5 He said me an interesting story about when he was a child.

Your score

/30

14.1

10 marks

What is each person doing? Write a sentence using one of the verbs from the box.

| carry | climb | dance | drive | fall | fly | jump | ride | ~~run~~ | swim | walk |

Example: He's running.

1 ....

2 ....

3 ....

4 ....

5 ....

6 ....

7 ....

8 ....

9 ....

10 ....

14.2

10 marks

Choose the correct word to complete each sentence. Circle the correct answer.

Example: We'll .... a bus to town.   a) arrive   (b) take)   c) go

1 Please could you .... me the bread.
  a) carry   b) pass   c) take

2 Please be quick or we'll .... the train.
  a) catch   b) take   c) miss

3 What time does the plane .... in Rome?
  a) arrive   b) fly   c) get

4 He can .... a bus.
  a) ride   b) drive   c) go

5 How did you .... to Paris?
  a) take   b) get   c) arrive

6 Can you .... a horse?
  a) drive   b) go   c) ride

7 Let's .... the underground.
  a) go   b) take   c) fly

8 If we run, we'll .... the bus.
  a) miss   b) go   c) catch

9 Pilots .... planes.
  a) fly   b) drive   c) ride

10 We can .... to Munich by train.
  a) take   b) pass   c) go

14.3

10 marks

Fill the gaps with the correct form of the words in the box (e.g. *go, goes* or *going*).

Example: I love ..going.. places by ship.

| carry | dance | drive | fall | fly | ~~go~~ | jog | ride | run | swim | walk |

1 At the sports club the children enjoy .... round the track, ... in the pool and .... their bikes.

2 You need a licence to .... a car or .... a plane.

3 On Friday evening we all go .... at a nightclub.

4 Bill likes to keep fit and every evening he puts on his tracksuit and .... for an hour before dinner.

5 Waiters get a lot of exercise. They .... miles every day as they .... food from the kitchen to the tables.

6 I don't like heights – I'm afraid of ....

15 Conjunctions and connecting words

15.1

Choose a word from the box to fill the gap in each sentence. Use each word once only.

when even also so before because and after if but

1 .... I went to sleep, I set my alarm clock for seven o'clock .... I had to get up early to go to the airport.
2 .... I win a lot of money one day, I'll stop working .... travel round the world.
3 This camera is so easy to operate; .... a child could take good pictures with it.
4 I like apples. I .... like oranges, ... I don't like bananas.
5 .... she left university she got a job in a computer company.
6 I'm going to study this evening, ... please don't phone me.
7 Phone me .... you get to London so that I know you are safe.

15.2 Choose the correct explanation. Circle the correct answer.

1 BOB: Although I love you, I don't want to marry you.
SALLY: Hmm.
a) Bob wants to marry Sally and he loves her.
b) Bob doesn't want to marry Sally but he loves her.
c) Bob doesn't love Sally and doesn't want to marry her.

2 HILDA: I'm like my sister in the face but I'm taller than her.
EVA: Really?
a) Hilda likes her sister's face although her sister is smaller.
b) Hilda's face is similar to her sister's and they are both the same height.
c) Hilda's face is similar to her sister's but her sister is smaller than her.

3 GEORGE: My brother and I both play the guitar but I play the violin too.
JOE: Oh yes.
a) George plays one more instrument than his brother.
b) George plays the violin and his brother plays the violin.
c) George only plays the violin; his brother only plays the guitar.

4 JESS: When I go to university I'll study maths.
RITA: Mm. Good.
a) Jess thinks it's possible he will go to university and study maths.
b) Jess prefers to study maths; he doesn't want to go to university.
c) Jess has decided he will go to university and study maths.

5 DENISE: Luke played the piano. He sang as well.
GUDRUN: Did he?
a) Luke played the piano and sang very well.
b) Luke played the piano and sang.
c) Luke played the piano but didn't sing.

15.3 Find five sentences that make sense in this table.

I'm going to study abroad	though so when if because	I've finished secondary school. I want to learn more about other countries and cultures. I can't speak any foreign languages. I will be away from home for three years. I get good grades in my exams.

16 Time words (1)

16.1

Which month is this?

Example: the 3rd month   <u>March</u>

1 the 6th month   ....
2 the 12th month   ....
3 the 8th month   ....
4 the 1st month   ....
5 the 7th month   ....
6 the 10th month   ....
7 the 2nd month   ....
8 the 9th month   ....
9 the 4th month   ....
10 the 11th month   ....

16.2

Match the words on the left with the definitions on the right.

1 afternoon	a	the day before today
2 century	b	Saturday and Sunday
3 day	c	the coldest season
4 evening	d	60 seconds
5 fortnight	e	7 days
6 minute	f	between 12 pm and 6 pm
7 tomorrow	g	24 hours
8 week	h	after 6 pm
9 weekend	i	the day after today
10 winter	j	14 days
11 yesterday	k	100 years

16.3

Fill the gap with the correct preposition.

Example: I had lunch with my aunt ...<u>on</u>............ Saturday.

1 Today is Monday. So the day .... tomorrow is Wednesday.
2 We had a lovely holiday .... the summer last year. We went to France ....
   July.
3 I am going to stay with Sophie .... the weekend. We are going to the cinema
   .... Friday evening and then we are going to visit my grandma .... Saturday.
4 There are seven days .... a week and 366 days .... a leap year.
5 We had an important meeting the day .... yesterday.
6 My brother's birthday is .... the spring.

17.1 Fill the gaps.

5 marks

1 It's four .... in the afternoon now.
2 Oscar came home at 2 pm. He came home two ....
3 Oscar has been home .... two ....

BILL'S HOLIDAY

17.2 Answer the questions.

5 marks

1 It's April now. Which month is next month?
2 Which month was last month?
3 Which month was it two months ago?
4 How long is Bill on holiday for?
5 It's Saturday April 16th today. What date will it be next Saturday?

17.3 How often? Put the words on the steps, from *not at all* to *every time*.

10 marks

sometimes	never
often	rarely
usually	now and then
always	occasionally
hardly ever	not often

EVERY TIME

NOT AT ALL

17.4 Now use the words on the right to fill the gaps in these sentences.

5 marks

1 Millie is afraid of flying so she has .... travelled
   on a plane in her life. She .... goes by train instead.   ALWAYS / NEVER
2 I meet him .... at the sports club, but I don't see
   him ....   OFTEN / NOW AND THEN
3 It .... snows in the south of the country. It ....
   rains instead, because it's warmer than the north.   USUALLY / HARDLY EVER
4   NINA: How often do you buy new clothes?
      RACHEL: Well, ... I'm a student, so I can only
                  afford to buy clothes ....   NOT OFTEN / OCCASIONALLY
5 .... I have no problem studying, but ....
   I start to feel sleepy if I read for a long time.   SOMETIMES / USUALLY

17.5 Complete the second sentence so that it means the same as the first one in each case.

5 marks

1 Right now, Ken takes the bus in the morning and again in the evening.
   .... the .... , Ken takes the bus .... a day.
2 I'll be back after a minute or so. See you in a very short time!
   I'll be back .... moment. See you .... !
3 Bill phones his sister every Friday. She was ill a short time ago.
   Bill phones his sister .... a week. She was ill ....
4 Many, many years ago, people used horses, not cars.
   In .... , people used horses, not cars.
5 Many, many years from now, people will travel to other planets for their holidays.
   In .... , people will travel to other planets for their holidays.

Your score

/30

18 Places

18.1

10 marks

Match these words with their opposites.

Example: at home – out

~~at home~~	back	beginning	bottom	end	front
here	left	~~out~~	right	there	top

18.2

10 marks

Look at the pictures and answer the questions.

Example: [A E I O U]   Which letter is in the middle?   ...I...

1 What is there on the front of the car?
2 What is there on the back of the car?
3 What is there on the side of the car?

4 What is at the top of the ladder?
5 Who is at the bottom of the ladder?
6 What is in the woman's right hand?
7 What is in the woman's left hand?

8 What is at the beginning of the path?
9 Who is in the middle of the path?
10 What is at the end of the path?

18.3

10 marks

Choose the best word from the box to fill each of the gaps in the e-mail.

abroad	~~at home~~	away	back	everywhere	here
left	middle	out	side	there	

Hi Mia,

I'm writing this from my computer ..at home.. . No one else is (1)..................... . The children are
(2)..................... at a friend's house and Will is (3)..................... for a few days. He's on business
(4)....................., in a small town in the (5)..................... of France. He'll be (6)..................... on Friday.
He's just sent me an e-mail to say that it's lovely and hot (7).....................! I can only see rain from the
window on my (8)..................... as I type and the TV says that it's raining (9)..................... in this country.
I wanted to plant some flowers at the (10)..................... of our house but it's too wet to be in the garden.
So I'm just going to read a book until it's time for the children to come home.

Love,
Tina

19.1 Put pairs of opposite words into the table.

10 marks

good	fast
quiet	sad
friendly	~~right~~
slow	bad
loud	unfriendly
~~wrong~~	happy

Opposites	
right	wrong

19.2 Fill the gaps with an adverb (e.g. *wrongly*) so that the second sentence means the same as the firs[t]

10 marks   *Example:* The numbers in this list are wrong.
                   This list is ..**wrongly**.... numbered.

1   He was driving at 140 kilometres per hour.
    He was driving very ....
2   He shouted her name.
    He said her name very ....
3   We went past the baby's bedroom, making very little noise because she was asleep.
    We went past the room very ....
4   He's a good pianist.
    He plays the piano really ....
5   There was ice on the road so we drove at 20 kilometres per hour.
    We drove very ....
6   She was very unfriendly when she spoke to us.
    She spoke to us .... very unfriendly ....
7   I don't swim for the school team because I'm a bad swimmer.
    I swim very ....
8   The little child smiled when he got his present because he was happy.
    He smiled ....
9   She looked at me in a very sad way.
    She looked at me very ....
10 Our teacher is always friendly when she corrects our mistakes.
    She always corrects our mistakes ....

19.3 Answer the questions using adverb forms of the words in the box. Write full sentences.

10 marks

sudden	impolite	strange	quick	easy

1   Harry said 'Shut your mouth!' to his teacher.
    How did Harry speak to his teacher?
2   Glen was acting in a way that no one could understand.
    How was Glen acting?
3   The accident happened in one short moment, and no one was expecting it.
    How did the accident happen?
4   Pippa passed the exam with no problems at all.
    How did she pass the exam?
5   He finished the job in less than a minute.
    How did he finish the job?

Your score

/30

20.1 Use the past tense forms of the verbs in the box to complete these sentences.

10 marks

Example: Jan ...*sang*......... a lovely song.

break	choose	drink	fly	meet	shine
shut	~~sing~~	spend	swim	throw	

1 The boy .... the ball.

2 The girl .... some milk.

3 The plane .... to Mexico.

4 Jack .... across the river.

5 The sun .... all day.

6 Rachel .... a glass.

7 Bill and Ben .... in town.

8 Anna .... a lot of money.

9 Joe .... the door.

10 Sam .... the biggest apple.

20.2 Complete this table.

10 marks

Infinitive	Past simple	Past participle
cut	*cut*	*cut*
	caught	
		forgotten
write		
	became	
		ridden

Infinitive	Past simple	Past participle
shoot		
	stole	
		begun
feel		
	stood	

20.3 Choose a verb from the table in 20.2 to complete these dialogues.

10 marks

Example: A: How did you feel yesterday?
B: I ...*felt*........... very tired so I went to bed early.

1 A: How did you get into town?
B: I .... a bus.

2 A: What's the matter?
B: I was preparing some vegetables and I .... my hand.

3 A: What did you do yesterday?
B: I .... a lot of letters and I .... reading a new book.

4 A: What happened in the film?
B: The bad guy .... a gun and .... the hero.

5 A: What is Jane doing now?
B: She has .... a nurse.

6 A: What did the children do in the park?
B: Jill .... her bike and Alex .... and watched her.

7 A: Isn't it cold today?
B: Yes – and I have .... to put on my hat.

21.1 Write the uncountable noun for each picture. We give you the first letter each time.

10 marks

1 i...........................

4 f...........................

2 a...........................

5 l...........................

3 w...........................

21.2 Put these nouns into two columns: countable and uncountable.

10 marks

| banana | milk | shoe | money | rice | bread |
| traffic | apple | bus | plate | butter | |

Countable	Uncountable
banana	

21.3 Correct the mistakes.

10 marks

1 Are these furnitures new? I haven't seen them before. (*2 marks*)
2 Our teacher gave us an advice about how to prepare for the exam.
3 We have ten people coming to lunch, so we'll need three large breads.
4 Here's your coffee. I have any sugar if you need it.
5 The traffics are always very bad around 8 o'clock in the morning.
6 The news are on TV in five minutes. Shall we watch them? (*2 marks*)
7 Rail travels are more interesting than going by air.
8 I have a lot of works to do before the exam next week.

Your score

/30

22 Common adjectives: good and bad things

22.1 Put these adjectives into the correct column.

10 marks

awful	best	better	brilliant	dreadful	excellent
fine	ghastly	gorgeous	great	horrendous	horrible
lovely	marvellous	nice	perfect	superb	terrible
wonderful	worse	worst			

Good	*Bad*
	awful

22.2 Circle the correct underlined adjective in these sentences.

10 marks

Example: Harry is a nice/(dreadful) man – nobody likes him.

1 I love Kay's new car – it's great/awful.
2 I don't like my boss – he's wonderful/horrible.
3 Let's go to Max's Restaurant tonight – the food there is ghastly/excellent.
4 Pete didn't enjoy the film – he said it was awful/superb.
5 Sue did very well in her test – the teacher said she wrote a terrible/brilliant essay.
6 The party was horrendous/lovely – everyone had a good time.
7 Thank you so much – I had a perfect/horrible day.
8 Jo does very well at school – she usually gets the best/worst marks in her class.
9 We're planning to have a picnic tomorrow – I hope the weather is fine/terrible.
10 The hotel was horrendous/gorgeous – we'll never go there again.

22.3 Fill the gaps in these dialogues. We give you the first letter each time.

10 marks

Example: A: I had a great time at the party last night.
B: ....Good.... !

1 A: Let's meet at 7– OK?
  B: P ....!
2 A: What dreadful weather!
  B: Yes, isn't it g............?
3 A: I'll send you a postcard from our holiday.
  B: L............!
4 A: The film was terrible, wasn't it!
  B: Yes, it was h............!
5 A: The food is good here, isn't it?
  B: Yes, it's m............!

6 A: I'll show you the town tomorrow.
  B: E............!
7 A: I don't like her very much, do you?
  B: No, she's a............!
8 A: I'll help you paint your room if you like.
  B: W............!
9 A: It's a beautiful view, isn't it?
  B: Yes, it's s............!
10 A: Did you enjoy the party?
  B: No, it was d............!

Your score

/30

23 Common adjectives: people

23.1
10 marks

Complete the table. Put a plus sign (+) if the adjective has a good/positive meaning, and a minus sign (−) if it has a bad/negative meaning.

Adjective	+ or −	Adjective	+ or −
stupid		lovely	
easy-going		happy	
selfish		horrible	
kind		nice	
difficult		intelligent	

23.2
10 marks

Use the adjectives from 23.1 to fill the gaps in these sentences. Use each adjective once only. We give you one of the letters in each word.

1 Julia is such a _ _ p _ _ person – she's always smiling and laughing.
2 Moira is a rather _ _ _ f _ _ _ person, always thinking about herself and what she wants.
3 Eva is an _ _ _ y-g _ _ _ _ sort of person; nothing ever worries her and she never panics.
4 What a h _ _ _ _ _ _ _ child! She hit that little girl and then ran off with her book!
5 I think you'll like Mr Barnes. He's _ _ c _ .
6 My grandfather is very _ _ n _ . He always gives me a present or some money when I visit him.
7 Gavin is the most _ n _ _ _ _ _ _ _ _ _ boy in the class. He always gets ten out of ten for his homework.
8 He knows she hates him but he asked her to marry him! What a _ t _ _ _ _ man!
9 My aunt can be a bit _ _ f _ _ _ _ _ _ . Everything is always a big problem for her.
10 Niall is an absolutely _ _ v _ _ _ person, so gentle and sweet; he does so many good things for his friends and family.

23.3
10 marks

Answer the questions.

1 Which adjective describes a child who is always good and does not do bad things?
2 Which adjective describes a child who is never good and does lots of bad things?
3 What is the opposite of *stupid*?
4 Fill the gap in this sentence with the correct preposition.
   'She was good/nice/wonderful .... me when I had problems.'
5 Fill the gap in this sentence with the correct preposition.
   'It was kind/good/nice .... you to help us yesterday.'

Your score
/30

Words and prepositions

24.1

10 marks

Match the sentence beginnings on the left with the endings on the right.

1 Wait at this stop	a for the lovely flowers.
2 Nurses look	b for our train tickets.
3 I'm looking forward	c at playing the violin.
4 She thanked him	d to a new job.
5 I'm not very interested	e for arriving late.
6 I'll pay	f for the number 10 bus.
7 The child is afraid	g in politics.
8 I must apologise	h for four cups of coffee.
9 Suzie is very good	i after people in hospital.
10 It can be hard to get used	j of big dogs.
11 James asked the waiter	k to the holidays.

24.2

10 marks

Fill the gaps in each sentence with the correct preposition.

Example: I won't be long. Please wait ..for.......... me.

1 I can't find my glasses. Can you help me look .... them?
2 Who does that car belong .... ?
3 Jane was very proud .... her son when he won first prize.
4 We're thinking .... going to Spain for our holiday.
5 Sally is bad .... maths but she is very good .... English.
6 I'm looking forward .... seeing you soon.
7 Dick apologised .... breaking the window.
8 Please look .... the statue on the right.
9 I'm not used .... getting up so early.

24.3

10 marks

Fill the gaps in this e-mail with verbs or adjectives.

Thanks for your e-mail. I [(1)] .... for not replying sooner, but I've been very
busy. I had a maths exam today. I'm not very [(2)] .... at maths, so I had to do a lot of work for it.
I have to [(3)] .... for my results – I won't get them for a week or two.

Now I'm free!!! This evening I'm going to [(4)] .... to a new CD which Mum bought me today.
We went to the shops together after my exam and I was going to [(5)] .... for it but Mum said
she'd buy it for me. She said she was [(6)] .... of me because I'd worked so hard for my exam.
I hope she feels the same when I get the results!

How are things with you? Have you got [(7)] .... to your new school yet? I liked the photo you
sent me. Does the skateboard you're standing on [(8)] .... to you? Aren't you [(9)] ....
of falling off?

I [(10)] .... forward to your next message.

Your score

/30

Bye for now,
Natasha

25 Prefixes

25.1

10 marks

Read the instructions. Use a prefix with the word on the left to complete the table.

Word	Instruction	Answer
possible	Make an adjective with the opposite meaning.	impossible
1 war	Make an adjective meaning 'before the war'.	
2 smoking	Make an adjective which means 'you must not smoke here'.	
3 price	Make an adjective that means '50% of the price'.	
4 send	Make a verb that means 'send something again'.	
5 girlfriend	Make a noun that means 'someone who was someone's girlfriend but is not any more'.	
6 happy	Make an adjective with the opposite meaning.	
7 comfortable	Make an adjective with the opposite meaning.	
8 tell	Make a verb that means 'tell something again'.	
9 formal	Make an adjective with the opposite meaning.	
10 finished	Make an adjective with the opposite meaning.	

25.2

10 marks

Rewrite the sentences using a word with the prefix given. Do not change the meaning.

Example: Mr Trottman is not popular with the students. (un)
   Mr Trottman is unpopular with the students.

1 He was the president of the club but he isn't any more. (ex)
2 I like wine that has no alcohol. (non)
3 I think you should write your essay again. (re)
4 He does not seem to be happy in his job. (un)
5 The restaurant has meals for children which cost only half the normal price. (half)
6 I don't like to give homework that I haven't finished to my teacher. (un)
7 The years before they start school are very important for little children. (pre)
8 It is not possible for anyone to live for 200 years. (im)
9 You can wear clothes that are not formal to the party. (in)
10 This chair is not comfortable. (un)

25.3

10 marks

Correct the mistakes.

1 This machine is insafe. Don't use it.
2 Every sentence in this section has something non-correct in it.
3 She is very unpolite to her teachers.
4 Do you ever get ex-exam nerves?
5 I still have some inread books from the library. I must read them.
6 The lessons are very unformal and we like the teacher very much.
7 Mike isn't my boss anymore. I have a new one. Mike is my pre-boss.
8 Years ago, you always had to say if you wanted a smoking or unsmoking seat on a plane.
9 It is only a halfhour drive from here to the airport.
10 I unaddressed the letter because it was for a person who had moved to a new address.

Your score

/30

26 Suffixes

26.1
10 marks

Look at the suffixes in the table. What do they mean? Add another example for each suffix.

	Suffix	*Meaning of suffix*	*Example*
hope<u>ful</u>, use<u>ful</u>, beauti<u>ful</u>	ful	full of	painful
1 work<u>er</u>, writ<u>er</u>, teach<u>er</u>, instruct<u>or</u>	er, or		
2 cook<u>er</u>, word process<u>or</u>, hair-dry<u>er</u>	er, or		
3 soci<u>ology</u>, bi<u>ology</u>, zo<u>ology</u>	ology		
4 use<u>less</u>, thought<u>less</u>, pain<u>less</u>	less		
5 happi<u>ness</u>, dark<u>ness</u>, kind<u>ness</u>	ness		

26.2
10 marks

Rewrite these sentences using an adverb ending in 'ly' instead of the adjective.

Example: The author of this book is a quick writer.
   <u>The author of this book writes quickly.</u>

1 Mike's a strong swimmer.
2 Jim's a slow walker.
3 The children are happy workers.
4 Paula's a beautiful dancer.
5 That footballer is a wonderful player.

26.3
10 marks

Put the letters in the right order to make a word and then match each phrase to the correct picture.

Example: They're studying T A I E S M M C H T A.   <u>mathematics – a</u>

1 They're studying I I L P S O C T.
2 It's a N U N Y S day.
3 It's a D A Y N S beach.
4 They're studying I C E O C M S N O.
5 It's a A I N Y R day.

a

c

e

b

d

f

27 Words you may confuse

27.1

10 marks

Circle the correct answer.

1 The opposite of *loud* is …
   a) quite.   b) quiet.
2 The past tense of *fall* is …
   a) felt.   b) fell.
3 The opposite of *tight* is …
   a) loose.   b) lose.
4 A *cooker* is …
   a) a person.   b) a thing.
5 The opposite of *find* is …
   a) loose.   b) lose.
6 The past tense of *feel* is …
   a) felt.   b) fell.
7 A police officer .... your driving licence.
   a) checks   b) controls
8 *Very* and .... can both be used before *big, small, nice*, etc.
   a) quiet   b) quite
9 If you need something, you can often .... it from a friend.
   a) lend   b) borrow
10 People stand at a bus stop to .... a bus.
   a) expect   b) wait for

27.2

10 marks

Choose a word from the box which ends in the same sound as the word in the table.

| shoes | belt | fight | diet | juice | ~~bell~~ |

Word	Same sound
fell	bell
1 quiet	
2 lose	
3 quite	
4 felt	
5 loose	

27.3

10 marks

Correct the mistakes in these sentences.

1 I borrowed her my pen and she never gave it back to me.
2 My brother is a really good cooker. I love eating at his house.
3 Yesterday I felt down the stairs and hurt my leg.
4 I haven't done enough work so I'm waiting to fail my exam.
5 Can I lend your tennis racket? I'll bring it back tomorrow.
6 They control your age before you can get into the nightclub. You must be 18.
7 I arrived at Rod and Fiona's house at 4.30 pm and said 'Good evening' to everyone.
8 I made some shopping yesterday and spent a lot of money.
9 Can you say me the way to the city centre?
10 Can you talk Spanish? What does 'loco' mean?

Your score

/30

28 Birth, marriage and death

28.1

10 marks

Circle the correct <u>underlined</u> word.

Example: Bill <u>is</u>/(was) born in London in 1972.

1 My parents <u>are/were</u> both born in Scotland in 1960.
2 Kay <u>got/went</u> married <u>to/with</u> Ben last Saturday.
3 After they get married they are going on <u>wedding/honeymoon</u> to Italy.
4 My grandparents were <u>marry/married</u> for 40 years.
5 His grandfather <u>dead/died</u> ten years ago.
6 He died <u>of/with</u> a heart attack on his 100th birthday.
7 They are going to <u>call/called</u> the baby Emily <u>from/after</u> her grandmother.
8 The old man became <u>ill/dead</u> last Sunday.

28.2

4 marks

Look at this form. What is the marital status of the people below?

Application form

What is your marital status?
Tick the correct box.

single ☐   widowed ☐

married ☐   divorced ☐

1 Pat's wife died last year. He is ....
2 Anna has a husband. She is ....
3 Polly's marriage has broken up. She is ....
4 Jim does not have a wife. He is ....

28.3

6 marks

Answer these questions about the picture.

1 What are the couple doing?   They are ....
2 What does the picture show?   A ....
3 Who is the woman?   The ....
4 Who is the man?   The ....
5 What is the word for the special holiday
  they will go on after this day?   The ....
6 What is the noun from *marry*?   m ....

28.4

10 marks

Complete these dialogues.

Example: A: Are you married?
           B: Yes.
           A: How long <u>have you been married?</u>
           B: Ten years already. I can't believe it!

1 A: Clare had a baby boy yesterday.
  B: How ....?
  A: 3 kilos.
  B: What are ....?
  A: Simon, I think. After Clare's father.
2 A: Jo's uncle is dead.
  B: Oh, I didn't know. When did he die?
  A: About a month ago.
  B: What ....?
  A: He had a heart attack, I think.

3 A: Did you enjoy the wedding?
  B: Yes, it was great.
  A: What ....?
  B: A long white dress.
  A: Where did they go ....?
  B: To France. They said it was fantastic.

Your score

/30

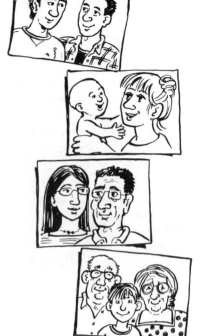

29.1 Complete what these people are saying.

10 marks

Example: I'm his brother, so he's also ...my brother...........

1 I'm her father, so she's ....

2 He's my mother's brother, so he's ....

3 I'm his mother, so he's ....

4 He's my brother, so I'm ....

5 I'm his daughter, so he's ....

6 She's my mother's mother, so she's ....

7 He's my son's son, so he's ....

8 He's my father's father, so he's ....

9 She's my mother's sister, so she's ....

10 They are my father's mother and father, so they're ....

29.2 Complete the crossword.

12 marks

Across

1 If you had only one child, would you
   like a son or a .... ?
2 Your uncle's son.
3 Mother and father together.

Down

4 Your mother's brother.
5 Girl with the same parents as you.
6 Your brother's daughters.

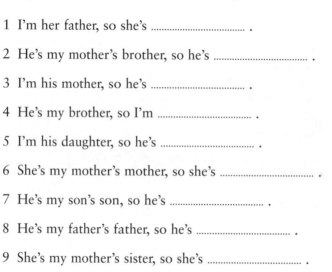

29.3 Are these statements correct? Circle the correct answer and correct any wrong sentences.

8 marks

1 My nephew John is my mother's sister's husband.   YES   NO

Your score

/30

2 My grandfather is my father's father.   YES   NO
3 Mary and David are married. Mary is David's husband.   YES   NO
4 I'm Philip, this is Nellie. We're married. She's my wife.   YES   NO

30.1

10 marks

First write the names of the body parts beside the pictures. Then find these parts of the body in the word square.

Example: .... tooth ....

1 ....
2 ....
3 ....
4 ....
5 ....
6 ....
7 ....
8 ....
9 ....
10 ....

A	T	M	T	O	O	T	H
S	H	O	U	L	D	E	R
T	U	U	N	E	C	K	F
O	M	T	N	M	O	M	I
M	B	H	O	P	A	R	N
A	G	E	S	A	L	E	G
C	A	R	E	K	N	E	E
H	E	A	R	T	I	P	R

30.2

14 marks

Answer these questions about the body.

Example: What do we have ten of on our feet?   toes

1 What do you see with and what do you hear with?
2 What two parts of your body do you regularly cut?
3 Which three parts of the body would someone measure before making a woman's evening dress?
4 What does the heart move round the body?
5 What part of the body controls what you do?
6 What is your whole body covered with?
7 On your foot you have your big toe. What do you have on your hand?
8 What part of the body do people often lie on when they sleep? Give two answers.
9 Is the 'ch' sound at the end of the word *stomach* pronounced like 'ch' in *church* or in *chemist*?

30.3

6 marks

Correct these sentences.

Example: John raised the weights above his bust.
          John raised the weights above his chest.

1 Her hairs are black.
2 Paul has a pain in the side.
3 John has broken two tooths.
4 Please wash the hands before dinner.
5 My foots hurt.
6 The children must put the hands up if they want to ask a question.

Your score

/30

31.1 Write the correct word under each picture.

10 marks

| skirt | belt | boots | socks | coat | hat | scarf | gloves | tie | shirt |

1 ....

3 ....

5 ....

7 ....

9 ....

2 ....

4 ....

6 ....

8 ....

10 ....

31.2 Underline the word on the right which has the same vowel sound as the word on the left.

5 marks

Example: shirt   red/<u>girl</u>/here

1 tie   tea/beer/why
2 gloves   rob/run/road
3 coat   note/not/mat
4 boots   foot/boat/shoot
5 scarf   off/half/at

31.3 Which five of these clothes words must always be used in the plural?

5 marks

| dresses | hats | trousers | jackets | tights | jeans | sweaters | shorts | shoes | sunglasses |

31.4 Answer the questions.

10 marks

1 Do you get dressed when you go to bed or when you get up?
2 What can you wear on your finger to show that you are married?
3 On which part of your body do you normally wear a hat?
4 What can you use to protect your eyes from the sun?
5 Who normally wears a dress – a man or a woman?
6 What do you call a jacket and trousers which you wear together?
7 What is another word for *sweater*?
8 Which is correct: 'Robert is wearing an umbrella / is carrying an umbrella / has an umbrella on'?
9 Which is correct: 'Lisa is using a skirt / Lisa has put a skirt on'?
10 What is another way of saying 'At night, I take my clothes off and go to bed'?

Your score

/ 30

32 Describing people

32.1

Put the words in the box into the correct column. Some words can go in more than one column.

| blue | tall | fair | thin | long | slim |
| green | short | brown | dark | fat | |

Eyes	Skin	Hair	Height and weight
blue			

32.2

Which sounds nicer? Underline the nicer sentence.

Example: <u>Cindy is beautiful</u>.   Cindy is pretty.

1 Sasha is slim.   Sasha is thin.
2 My boss is old.   My boss is elderly.
3 My brother is handsome.   My brother is ugly.
4 Tamara is ordinary-looking. Tamara is pretty.
5 Pat is overweight.   Pat is fat.

32.3

Answer these questions using the opposites.

Example: Is your cat old?   <u>No, she's young</u>.

1 Has your sister got long, fair hair?
2 Is your aunt short and overweight?
3 Is your dog young?
4 Is your uncle ugly?
5 Has your mother got fair hair?
6 Is your brother thin?
7 Is your little sister pretty?
8 Is your cousin tall?

32.4

Complete the five sentences describing this man.

Example: He's got ...brown............ eyes.

1 He's got a ....
2 He's also got a ....
3 His skin is ....
4 He's got .... hair.
5 He is ....

TEST

33 Health and illness

33.1

10 marks

Match the sentences on the left with the sentences on the right.

1	I feel sick.	a	I'm going to ring the dentist.
2	I'm fine.	b	I think I should call a doctor.
3	I've got toothache.	c	I think I'll go home and rest.
4	I feel really ill.	d	I think I ate something bad.
5	I don't feel very well.	e	I feel very well.

33.2

5 marks

Say the words aloud, then write them down.

Example: /ˈdɒktə/   *doctor*

1 /ˈhedeɪk/ ....
2 /məˈleəriə/ ....
3 /ˈæsmə/ ....
4 /ˈkænsə/ ....
5 /ˈkɒlərə/ ....

33.3

5 marks

Match the sentences below with the illnesses from 33.2.

1 Bad drinking water can cause it.
2 This makes it hard to breathe.
3 Smoking can cause it.
4 It's difficult to study when you have one.
5 You can get it from a mosquito bite.

33.4

10 marks

Fill the gaps. Sometimes you are given the first and/or last letter.

1 I have a lot of s...................... in my job, so when I get home, I try to r......................x and not think about work.
2 My uncle Tim had a heart a...................... and he's in h...................... .
3 Every summer I get h...................... ; the flowers and grass make me s...................... .
4 I try to have a good, healthy d...................... with lots of fruit and vegetables.
5 E...................... is very important, for example, jogging, swimming, cycling.
6 If you've got a c......................d it's a good idea to stay at home and go to bed with a hot drink.
7 If you have a headache it may help if you take an ....n.

Your score

/30

36 *Test Your English Vocabulary in Use (Elementary)*

34.1 How do you feel? Choose the best word from the box.

10 marks

Example: You've just had a long holiday with lots of good food and exercise.
          <u>You feel well.</u>

angry	cold	happy	hot	hungry	ill
sad	surprised	thirsty	tired	~~well~~	

1 You haven't eaten for ten hours.
2 You went to bed at 2 am and got up at 6 am.
3 Someone has just broken a window in your new car.
4 It is a hot day and you haven't had anything to drink for three hours.
5 You have a very bad cold.
6 It is snowing and you do not have a coat with you.
7 You got very good marks in an important exam.
8 It is 35°C and you do not have air conditioning.
9 Your dog has just died.
10 You see your brother's photo on the front page of the newspaper.

34.2 What are the opposites of these verbs and adjectives?

5 marks

Example: good   <u>bad</u>

1 like   2 love   3 cold   4 happy   5 ill

34.3 Rewrite the sentences using the words in brackets.

5 marks

Example: Peter dislikes his new boss. (like)
          <u>Peter doesn't like his new boss.</u>

1 I don't like abstract paintings. (dislike)
2 I hope my brother gets a new job. (want)
3 Jack wants his girlfriend to phone him soon. (hope)
4 I like strawberry ice cream more than vanilla ice cream. (prefer)
5 My little sister prefers juice to milk. (likes)

34.4 How do these people look? Use the letters to make a word and finish the sentence.

10 marks

Example: The woman with short hair looks O T H.
          <u>The woman with short hair looks hot.</u>

1 The tall girl looks T U S E P.
2 The fat man looks G A R Y N.
3 The old man looks D A S.
4 The short girl looks L I L.
5 The thin man looks P E S S I D U R R.
6 The boy with dark hair looks M R A W.
7 The boy with fair hair looks D I R T E.
8 The woman with long hair looks P A P H Y.
9 The dog looks R I T T Y S H.
10 The cat looks G H U R Y N.

Greetings and other useful phrases

35.1 **What do you say?**

10 marks

1 You arrive at someone's office at 10 am.   Good ....

2 You arrive at someone's house at 8 pm.   Good ....

3 You lift your glass before starting a drink
   with a group of people.   .... everybody!

4 You want to get off a bus but there are
   people in your way.   .... , please.

5 Someone sneezes.   .... !

35.2 **Fill the gaps in the conversation with these phrases.**

10 marks

not too bad, thanks	goodbye	and you	hi	congratulations
how are you	see you soon	happy birthday	good luck	hello

RON: .... , Fiona.

FIONA: .... , Ron.

RON: .... ?

FIONA: Fine. .... ?

RON: .... It's my birthday today.

FIONA: Oh! .... !

RON: Thanks. So, how's university?

FIONA: Oh, great. In fact I just passed a big exam.

RON: Oh good! .... !

FIONA: Thanks. The only problem is I've got another one next week.

RON: Really? Oh well, ... !

FIONA: Thanks. Well, I must go now. Are you going to Anne's party on Saturday?

RON: Yeah. Well, ... , then.

FIONA: Yes. .... , see you at the party.

RON: Bye.

35.3 **Correct the mistakes in these conversations.**

10 marks

1   LIM: Chinese New Year starts this week.
      DEREK: Oh really? Merry New Year!

2   DIANE: Here's the newspaper you asked me to get.
   NORBERT: Please.
      DIANE: No problem.

3   RUTH: This is my last day in the office till December 28th.
        WILL: Oh, well, I'll say Good Christmas, then.
       RUTH: Thanks. You too.

4   GEOFF: I swam a kilometre today.
        FRAN: Well made! You must be very fit.
      GEOFF: Yeah, I feel good.

5   BETH: It's my birthday today.
      SONYA: Oh, congratulations!
       BETH: Thank you.

Your score

/30

Countries, languages and people

36.1
10 marks
Which continent are these countries in?

Example: Thailand   Thailand is in Asia.

Afghanistan	Argentina	Brazil	China	Egypt
Ethiopia	Finland	Germany	Italy	Japan
Libya	Canada	Mongolia	Paraguay	Russia
Singapore	Slovakia	Spain	~~Thailand~~	USA
Zimbabwe				

36.2
10 marks
Complete this table.

Country	Adjective	Language
France	French	French
The Netherlands (Holland)		
Iceland		
Iraq		
Korea		
Norway		
Peru		
Portugal		
Saudi Arabia		
Switzerland		
Thailand		

36.3
10 marks
Where are these capital cities? Write a sentence about each city. You can use an atlas to help you.

Example: Brussels

Brussels is the capital of Belgium.

1 Ottawa
2 Santiago
3 Athens
4 Budapest
5 Caracas
6 Ankara
7 Montevideo
8 Kathmandu
9 Stockholm
10 Damascus

Your score

/30

37 Weather

37.1 Match the weather words on the left with the sentences on the right.

10 marks

1	rain	a	You can't see it but it makes things move about.
2	sun	b	It makes a very loud noise.
3	thunder	c	When light comes suddenly from the sky, often during a storm.
4	fog	d	It's yellow and makes you feel warm.
5	snow	e	Water falls from the sky.
6	lightning	f	These are sometimes big and white and can be seen in the sky.
7	clouds	g	It's a very strong wind.
8	wind	h	It's white and cold.
9	storm	i	It's a strong wind and heavy rain together.
10	hurricane	j	You can't see things in the distance.

37.2 If the adjective form ends in 'y', write it in the box. If it does not, put an X in the box.

10 marks

	Noun	Adjective
1	fog	
2	sun	
3	lightning	
4	thunder	
5	wind	
6	hurricane	
7	snow	
8	rain	
9	thunderstorm	
10	cloud	

37.3 Correct the mistakes.

10 marks

1 What a lovely weather! Shall we go to the beach?
2 It's snowing in New York and fogging in Chicago today.
3 It's very wet in the Sahara Desert. It hardly ever rains there.
4 We had a stormthunder last night. It woke me up.
5 It was raining and winding so we stayed at home.

Your score

/30

38.1 What do these signs mean?

5 marks

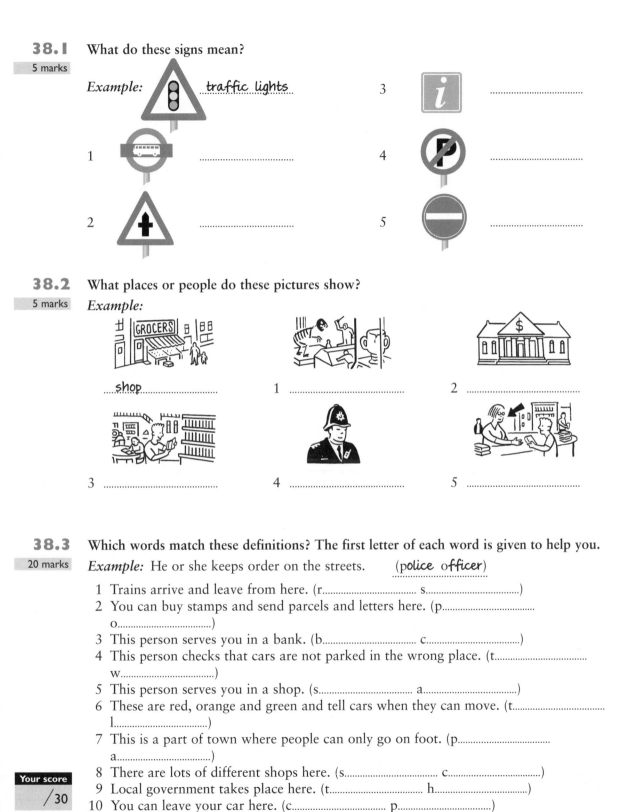

Example: ..traffic lights..

1 ....

2 ....

3 ....

4 ....

5 ....

38.2 What places or people do these pictures show?

5 marks

Example:

....shop............

1 ....

2 ....

3 ....

4 ....

5 ....

38.3 Which words match these definitions? The first letter of each word is given to help you.

20 marks

Example: He or she keeps order on the streets. (police officer)

1 Trains arrive and leave from here. (r........................... s.............................)

2 You can buy stamps and send parcels and letters here. (p...........................
o...............................)

3 This person serves you in a bank. (b............................... c.........................)

4 This person checks that cars are not parked in the wrong place. (t...........................
w...............................)

5 This person serves you in a shop. (s............................... a...........................)

6 These are red, orange and green and tell cars when they can move. (t...........................
l...............................)

7 This is a part of town where people can only go on foot. (p...............................
a...............................)

8 There are lots of different shops here. (s............................... c.........................)

9 Local government takes place here. (t........................... h...........................)

10 You can leave your car here. (c........................... p...........................)

Your score

/30

39.1 Match the words on the left with the definitions on the right.

10 marks

1 farm		a	large area full of trees
2 lake		b	smaller than a town
3 mountain		c	small house in the country
4 village		d	large area of water
5 hill		e	smaller than a road, not for cars
6 forest		f	the Thames, the Amazon and the Nile are examples
7 path		g	place where people keep animals and grow food
8 field		h	there are a lot of these in the Alps and in the Himalayas
9 cottage		i	closed piece of land where animals live or people grow food
10 river		j	high ground, but not as high as the Alps or Himalayas

39.2 Use the words from 39.1 to fill the gaps. Use each word once only. Sometimes you will have

10 marks   to use the plural form.

1 She lives in a small .... of about 500 people.
2 We got out of the car and walked along a .... by the river.
3 If we cut down more and more trees there will be no .... left in the world.
4 The .... goes through three countries and then into the Mediterranean Sea.
5 The town has .... all round it; some of them are 3,000 metres high.
6 They have a house near a .... and have a boat they can use on it.
7 He has a little .... in the country, where he spends the weekends.
8 There were some sheep in the .... , eating the grass.
9 I lived on a .... when I was a child. I loved the animals and the open air.
10 The east of England is good for cycling holidays because there are not many ....

39.3 Correct the mistakes. There may be more than one in each sentence.

10 marks

1 I love the nature, so when I finish my studies I'm going to work in a conservatory area in the countryside.
2 In the summer we go to the mountains for picnics; in the winter we go there for ski.
3 At the weekends, I like to get out of the city and go for a walk in the nature.
4 There are some fantastic wildlifes in the national park.
5 He lives in a beautiful house in the mountain.
6 Athens is a country in the city of Greece.
7 I'm reading a book about a man who has climbed all the highest hills in the Himalayas.
8 We live in the countryside and go walk most weekends.

Animals and pets

40.1
10 marks

What are these animals?

Example:  sheep

1 ....

2 ....

3 ....

4 ....

5 ....

6 ....

7 ....

8 ....

9 ....

10 ....

40.2
10 marks

Which animal word matches these definitions?

Example: a young hen   chick

1 a young horse
2 the meat from a hen
3 a green, yellow or blue bird that can be a pet
4 young birds, tortoises and snakes are all born from these
5 we get this from sheep and use it to make warm clothes
6 the meat from a pig (*2 words*)
7 we drink this and also use it to make cheese and butter
8 a long thin animal with no legs
9 the skin of cows – we use it to make shoes and handbags

40.3
10 marks

Which word does not belong in each group? Explain.

Example: hen, monkey, parrot, budgie
             Monkey – because the others are all birds.

1 lion, tiger, horse, cat
2 elephant, giraffe, snake, cow
3 calf, lamb, sheep, piglet
4 fish, tortoise, dog, pig
5 beef, foal, ham, chicken

Your score

/30

Travelling

41.1

10 marks

Write the type of transport under each picture.

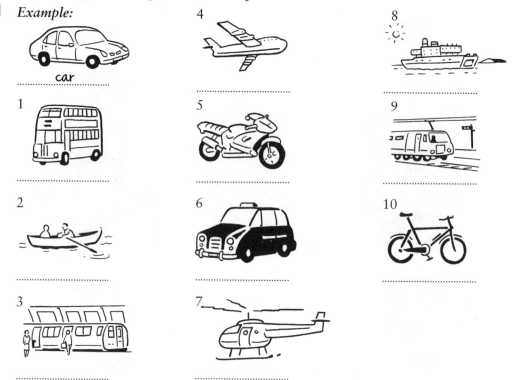

Example:

car

1

2

3

4

5

6

7

8

9

10

41.2

10 marks

Answer the questions.

1 You want to find out where a place is. What can you look at?
2 What do you need to show when you arrive in a new country?
3 In which part of the train can you buy food / have a meal?
4 A ticket from A to B and back again is a *return* ticket. What do we call a ticket from A to B only?
5 Who checks your suitcases and other bags when you arrive in a new country?
6 What word means 'suitcases and other bags'?
7 What can you look at to find the times of buses or trains?
8 You need a car for your holiday but don't want to use your own car. What can you do?
9 What type of card do you need to get on a plane?
10 What do you call the people who work on the plane and bring you meals, etc.?

41.3

10 marks

Circle the correct answer.

1 The plane   (a) grounded   (b) took down   (c) landed   at 6.35.

2 I need to   (a) fill   (b) tank   (c) put   up my car. Is there a petrol station near here?

3 The train has just arrived   (a) by   (b) in   (c) at   platform number 5.

Your score

/30

4 The officer   (a) controlled   (b) checked   (c) looked   my passport and said 'Welcome to Bolania.'

5 I'm going near your house. Can I give you a   (a) lift   (b) drive   (c) carry?

42.1 What must you do / not do or what can you do if you see these notices?

10 marks

Example: WAY IN You can go in that door.

1 EXIT

2 PULL

3 Open

4 *Please do not walk on the grass*

5 *Queue this side*

6 SALE

7 *out of order*

8 Please pay here

9 Please ring for attention

10

42.2 Fill in these notices.

5 marks

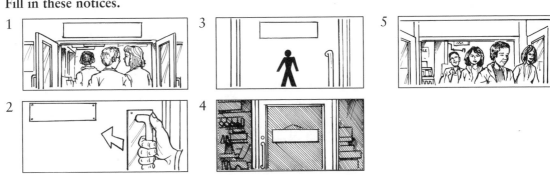

1   3   5

2   4

42.3 Write the notices that you need in these situations.

15 marks

Example: You have just planted some new grass and do not want people to walk on it.
Please do not walk on the grass.

1 You work in a shop and you are going to sell some things very cheaply.
2 You want to show that there is a toilet behind the door (*2 marks*)
3 You want to show that a door moves away from the person using it.
4 You work in a café and it is now time for staff to go home.
5 You work in a café and you do not want people to smoke there.
6 You want to show that a door moves towards the person using it.
7 You work in reception at a hotel and want people to use a bell to let you know they are there.
8 You want people to use this door to leave a cinema. (*2 marks*)
9 You work in a café and the public phone you have there is not working.
10 You want people to use this door to go into a cinema. (*2 marks*)
11 You work in a shop and want to show people where to pay.
12 You work in a shop and want to show people how to queue when they want to pay.

Your score
/30

43 Food and drink

43.1 Complete the two crosswords with the names of the fruit and vegetables in the pictures.

10 marks

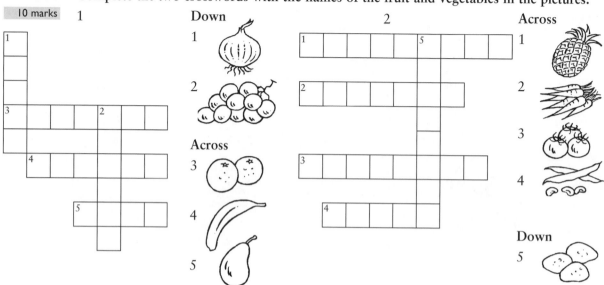

43.2 Use the words from 43.1 to fill the gaps in the sentences. The first letter is given.

10 marks

1 P............................ have a very hard skin and are difficult to cut, but the fruit is delicious.
2 O............................ always make my eyes water when I peel them.
3 When t............................ are red, they are ready to eat.
4 A b............................ is a good, healthy snack; fruit is better for you than sweets.
5 We use p............................ to make chips.
6 P............................ grow on trees, and are ready to eat in the autumn.
7 Green b............................ are a popular vegetable and are very good for you.
8 O............................ are often used to make juice.
9 You don't have to cook c............................ . They are very nice to eat raw.
10 Red g............................ and green ones are both used to make wine.

43.3 Complete the conversations using words from the list. Use each word once only.

10 marks

fish   pasta   pizza   fruit juice   wine   garlic   peas   strawberries   hamburgers   hot-dogs

1   EDITH: Are you a vegetarian?
    SYLVIE: Not really. I don't eat meat but I do eat .... because we live near
    the sea.
2 CARMEN: Do they only sell beer in British pubs?
      JOE: No, they sell .... too, and non-alcoholic drinks such as ....
3   VERA: What types of fast food do you like?
    RITA: Oh, everything, ... , ... , ...
4 KIERA: What's your favourite fruit?
   DONNA: .... I just love them! Especially with cream or ice cream!
5 NURDAN: Are there any vegetables you don't like?
    JANE: I don't like .... It's too strong for me, and I don't like the smell.
6   LISA: What shall we have with the fish? Potatoes?
   HENRY: Mmm, I'd prefer .... or rice.
    LISA: Okay, what about vegetables? There are some frozen .... in the freezer.
   HENRY: Yes, fine.

44 In the kitchen

44.1

10 marks

Complete the dialogue.

MARY: I've got some tomatoes out of the 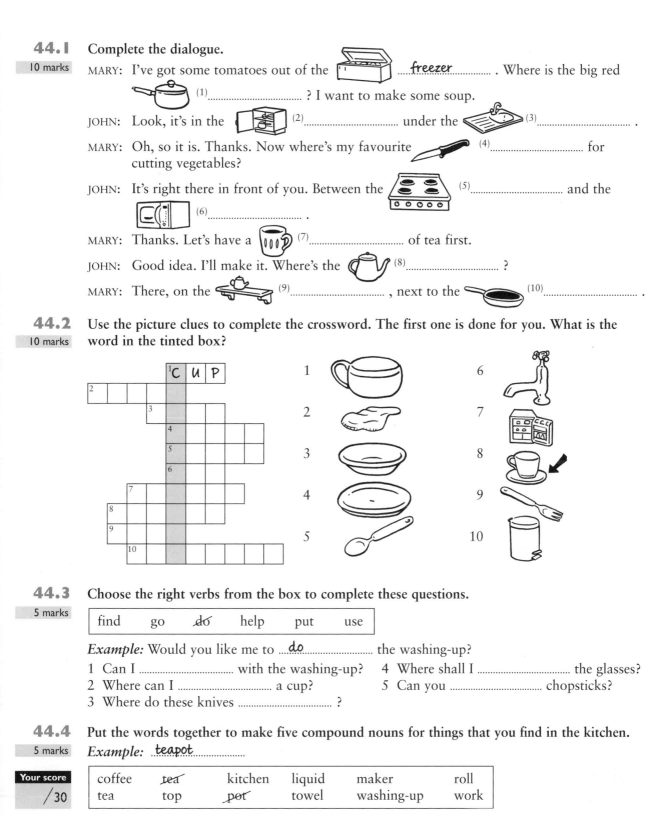 ....*freezer*......... . Where is the big red
(1)............................ ? I want to make some soup.

JOHN: Look, it's in the (2)............................ under the (3)............................ .

MARY: Oh, so it is. Thanks. Now where's my favourite (4)............................ for
cutting vegetables?

JOHN: It's right there in front of you. Between the (5)............................ and the
(6)............................ .

MARY: Thanks. Let's have a (7)............................ of tea first.

JOHN: Good idea. I'll make it. Where's the (8)............................ ?

MARY: There, on the (9)............................ , next to the (10)............................ .

44.2

10 marks

Use the picture clues to complete the crossword. The first one is done for you. What is the
word in the tinted box?

44.3

5 marks

Choose the right verbs from the box to complete these questions.

find	go	~~do~~	help	put	use

Example: Would you like me to ....*do*............... the washing-up?
1 Can I .... with the washing-up?   4 Where shall I .... the glasses?
2 Where can I .... a cup?   5 Can you .... chopsticks?
3 Where do these knives .... ?

44.4

5 marks

Put the words together to make five compound nouns for things that you find in the kitchen.
Example: ....*teapot*...............

Your score
/30

coffee	~~tea~~	kitchen	liquid	maker	roll
tea	top	~~pot~~	towel	washing-up	work

45 In the bedroom and bathroom

45.1 Match the words with the pictures.

10 marks

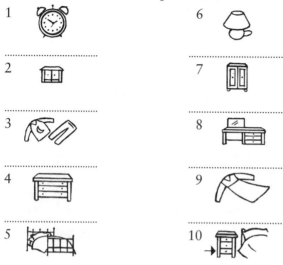

1

2

3

4

5

6

7

8

9

10

| bedside table |
| wardrobe |
| chest of drawers |
| cupboard |
| bed |
| dressing table |
| alarm clock |
| pyjamas |
| nightdress |
| bedside lamp |

45.2 Match the words with the pictures.

10 marks

| bath | shampoo | toilet | towel | shelf |
| soap | shower | basin | toothbrush | toothpaste |

1 ....

2 ....

3 ....

4 ....

5 ....

6 ....

7 ....

8 ....

9 ....

10 ....

45.3 Correct the mistakes.

10 marks

Your score

/30

Every morning, when my alarm clock calls I awake up. Then I go up and have a shower and be dressed. I go downstairs and have breakfast. Then I go back to the bathroom and wash my teeth. At the end of the day, at about 11.30, I go upstairs, go undressed and go in bed. I listen the radio for a while then I turn the light and go to asleep.

46 In the living room

46.1
10 marks

Choose words from the box to match the descriptions.

armchair	book	bookshelf	carpet	chair
coffee table	curtains	desk	light	light switch
music centre	CD player	~~phone~~	phone book	power point
radio	reading lamp	remote control	sofa	table
TV				

Example: You can talk to people on this. ..phone..

1 You sit on this. (3 words)
2 You walk on this.
3 You often find books on this. (4 words)
4 You can listen to this. (4 words)
5 You need this when it gets dark (3 words)
6 You can turn the TV on and off with this.
7 You turn the light off with this.
8 You can read this. (2 words)
9 You need this for electrical things.

46.2
16 marks

Write the number beside each object and draw a line from it to the right place in the picture.

...... Example ......

Example: Put the phone on the armchair.
1 Put the TV in the corner next to the door.
2 Put the remote control on the sofa.
3 Put the picture on the wall near the window.
4 Put the CD player next to the power point.
5 Put the radio on the bookshelf.
6 Put the reading lamp on the table.
7 Put the book under the chair.
8 Put the light switch on the wall next to the door.

46.3
4 marks

Complete each sentence with a verb.

Example: It's too dark in here. Could you ..switch.. the light ..on.. , please?
1 It'll soon be dark. It's time to .... the curtains.
2 I'd like to talk to you. Can you .... the TV .... , please?
3 I always like to .... the news on TV.
4 When I want to .... after work, I lie on the sofa and listen to music.

Your score
/30

47 Jobs

47.1

What do we call ...

1 ... a person who cuts your hair?
2 ... a person who works in an office and writes letters, answers the phone, etc.?
3 ... a person who lives in the country and grows food and/or keeps animals for food?
4 ... a person you go to when you are ill, who examines you, decides what is wrong and gives you medicine?
5 ... a person who designs and builds bridges, roads, etc.?
6 ... a person who mends cars and other machines?
7 ... a person who serves you in a restaurant?
8 ... a person who cares for sick people in a hospital but is not a doctor?
9 ... a person who gives you lessons?
10 ... a person who works in a shop?

47.2

Now use the words from 47.1 to fill the gaps. Use each word once only. Sometimes you will have to use the plural form.

1 The .... said it would cost €300 to fix my car.
2 I went for a walk in the countryside and met a .... looking after some sheep.
3 Do you like my hair? I have a new .... I think she's better than the old one.
4 Our .... said we're going to have a grammar test next Monday.
5 You can't talk to the director but you can leave a message with his ....
6 While I was studying I worked as a .... in a big store at weekends.
7 I like the idea of building big bridges and motorways, so I'd like to be an ....
8 To become a .... you have to study medicine for five years.
9 The .... were very kind to me when I was in hospital. They were always there when I needed them.
10 The .... in that restaurant are very friendly.

47.3

True or false? Write T for true, F for false. If you write F, say why.

1 A bus driver works in an office. ....
2 'What do you do?' is another way of saying 'What is your job?'. ....
3 A person who drives a taxi is called a taxman. ....
4 A person who writes books is called a writer. ....
5 If you do your job/profession in your own house or flat, you can say 'I work at home' or 'I work from home.' Both are correct. ....
6 It is correct to say 'I have an interesting work.' ....
7 Cars are made in a factory. ....
8 If someone asks you about your job, you can say 'I'm teacher.' ....
9 A person who repairs cars is called a mechanician. ....
10 Doctors and nurses work in hospitals. ....

Your score

/30

At school and university

48.1 Which school subject is each person talking about?

10 marks

Example: CARLOS: 'I need it because I want to study in Australia one day.'   English

1   MARK: 'It's my favourite subject because I love learning about other countries.'
2   SIMONE: 'I like it because I love drawing and painting pictures.'
3   KIM: 'I think it is very interesting to learn about animals and plants.'
4   TESSA: 'It's good because we run and jump and aren't sitting at a desk.'
5   ABDUL: 'Numbers are very interesting and I love working with them.'
6   ALEX: 'I love learning about how people lived in the past.'
7   DINA: 'I think it is very important to learn all about computers.'
8   MARIA: 'We study speed and light and movement – it's great.'
9   PAT: 'We learn songs and sometimes we can play instruments.'
10 MEENA: 'I enjoy doing experiments in the lab with different chemicals.'

48.2 What are these things called? Put the letters in order to make words and then match the

10 marks

words with the pictures.

Example: ENP   pen – a

1   POH
2   RADOB
3   LURRE
4   KNOOTBEO
5   APERP PILC
6   BURREB
7   TESACEST
8   GNARIWD IPN
9   CENOTI RADOB
10 PLINCE PHENARRES

48.3 Complete each sentence with a verb in the correct form (e.g. *get, got, getting*).

10 marks

Example: At the end of a university course, you ...get............ a degree.

1   Mary likes school but she hates .... homework.
2   Professor Brown is .... a lecture on Shakespeare this afternoon.
3   While the lecturer speaks, the students .... notes.
4   Children usually .... to ride a bike at the age of six or seven.
5   My brother is .... a course in computing this weekend.
6   When my English course .... I have to .... an exam.
7   Everyone hopes to .... their exams; no one wants to ....
8   Mr Jones .... my son history.

49.1

6 marks

Here are six things we use to help us communicate. Put the letters in order to make words.

1 KYDBROAE   k.....................................
2 TETERL   l.....................................
3 LIEBOM HONEP   m................................. ....
4 STOP BXO   p............................... ....
5 PONTELEHE   t.....................................
6 CREESN   s.....................................

49.2

10 marks

Fill the gaps in the conversations.

1   RORY: What's your .... ?
    COLIN: It's 26, Park Road, Shilton, SH4 6BC.
2   TERRY: I'll ring you at ten o'clock tomorrow.
    MIKE: Okay, if I'm not at home leave a message on my ....
3   (In a restaurant)
    ROB: Is there a phone .... near here? I have to make a call.
    WAITER: Yes, sir, there's one on the corner, go out and turn left.
4   (Sitting at a computer)
    GARRY: How do I close this program?
    LINDA: Use the .... to click on 'EXIT' in the top corner of the screen.
5   (Working at Anne's computer)
    DANA: I want to save my work and take it to college tomorrow. Can you lend me a
    .... ?
    ANNE: Yes, sure, there's a box of them next to the computer.

49.3

10 marks

Put these sentences into the correct order to make a typical phone conversation.

He's not here right now. Who's calling?
Hello, seven six three double-eight five.
Okay, I'll tell him.
Hi, can I speak to Ken?
Bye.
It's Joanna. Could you give him a message?
No problem. Bye.
Yeah.
Thanks.
Could you tell him I called and I'll call back later.

49.4

4 marks

Write questions for these answers. Use the words in brackets.

1 It's the same as my phone number, 378654. (fax)
2 It's Bob dot Jones at Freemail dot com. (e-mail)
3 Yes, of course you can. The phone is in the kitchen. (make)
4 24th March. (date, letter)

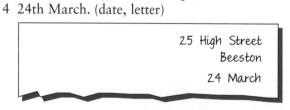

25 High Street
Beeston
24 March

Your score

/30

50 Holidays

50.1

10 marks

Answer these questions.

Example: What kind of sport is skiing?   <u>a winter sport</u>

1 What kind of cheques can you use in any country?
2 What do you need to buy if you want to go on a bus, plane or train?
3 What are dollars, euros and yen examples of?
4 What do you call a holiday when you pay for everything (travel, hotel, etc.) together?
5 If a town has a lot of restaurants, discos and nightclubs, you can say that the .... is good.
6 What do you call all the things that you take with you on holiday?
7 What do you call a book that tells you lots of useful holiday expressions in another language?
8 What do people usually send their friends when they are on holiday?
9 Where do you go if you are in a new town and you want to know about local sights and hotels?
10 What kind of boat can you take your car on?

50.2

5 marks

Correct the mistakes in these sentences.

Example: Take your currency so you can take photos when you're on holiday.
<u>Take your camera so you can take photos when you're on holiday.</u>

1 A coach is a large comfortable train.
2 When you go into another country, they look at your phrase book.
3 You are only allowed to visit some countries if you have a special postcard.
4 A ferry takes you across land.
5 When you go camping, you sleep in a hotel.

50.3

15 marks

Fill in the gaps in this dialogue.

RICK: Have you been ..<u>on</u>.......................... holiday this year yet, Meg?
MEG: Yes, we (1)................................... a fantastic holiday in Russia last month.
RICK: Great! How did you get there?
MEG: We (2)........................ from London to Finland and then we took a (3)...................................
across the Baltic Sea from Helsinki to St Petersburg. We spent a couple of days there
and then we went to Moscow (4).................................. bus. We came home from Moscow
(5).................................. train.
RICK: So, what was it like? What did you think of the local (6).................................. ?
MEG: It was delicious! And there was lots of excellent (7).................................. – very good discos
and clubs, all open till very late.
RICK: Do you (8).................................. any Russian?
MEG: No, but we had a good (9).................................. and that helped us a lot. What about you,
Rick?
RICK: We're (10).................................. on holiday next week. We're going to (11)..................................
camping. We love sleeping in a (12).................................. and it's very easy. We're going in
our own (13).................................. and we're staying in this country so, of course, we can
just use our ordinary money – we don't need to take any (14).................................. or foreign
(15).................................. .

MEG: Well, I hope you have a wonderful time!

51 Shops and shopping

51.1

Which type of shop would you go to ...

1 ... to buy meat?
2 ... to buy things for little children to play with?
3 ... to buy bread and cakes?
4 ... to buy a present for someone?
5 ... to buy food and everyday things for your house?
6 ... to buy medicines and personal items?
7 ... to buy newspapers and magazines?
8 ... to buy stamps?
9 ... to have your hair cut?
10 ... to buy books?

51.2

Which department in a big store would you go to if you were looking for these things?

1 ....   5 ....

2 ....   6 ....

3 ....   7 ....

4 ....   8 ....

51.3

Fill the gaps in the conversations.

1 CUSTOMER: The .... said I could change it as long as I kept the ....

2 CUSTOMER: Where can I pay for this, please?
SHOP ASSISTANT: You can pay at that .... over there.

3 SHOP ASSISTANT: Can I .... you, madam?
CUSTOMER: Yes, how much does this hat .... ?
SHOP ASSISTANT: Oh, let's see. Here we are – €35.

4 (In a small café)
CUSTOMER: Can I pay by .... card?
WAITER: Sorry, sir, we don't have a machine.
CUSTOMER: Oh. Can I write a .... ?
WAITER: No, I'm very sorry, sir, ... only. This is just a small café.

5 SALLY: I like this sweater. Shall I buy it?
MARY: Why don't you .... it on first and see how it looks on you?
SALLY: Yes, maybe I should.

6 (The customer has just bought a scarf)
SHOP ASSISTANT: There you are, madam. $25, and here's your .... , $5. Shall I put it in a .... for you?
CUSTOMER: No thanks. I'll put it on. It's cold today!

7 CUSTOMER: I bought this jacket yesterday. It's too big for me. Do you have it in a smaller .... ?

52.1 Name these things.

10 marks

Example: .... TV ....

1 ....
2 ....
3 ....
4 ....
5 ....

6 ....
7 ....
8 ....
9 ....
10 ....

52.2 Choose a verb from the box to complete these sentences.

10 marks

Example: Could I ..exchange.......... some money, please?

| book | cash | change | check | check out | ~~exchange~~ |
| fill in | get | have | have | sign | |

1 I .... a reservation for a double room for tonight.
2 Please could you .... this form?
3 Please .... your name at the bottom of the form.
4 .... your bill carefully before you pay it.
5 Could I .... breakfast in my room, please?
6 To .... an outside line, you should dial 0.
7 I'd like to .... a traveller's cheque, please.
8 I would like to .... a room for next weekend, please.
9 Could I .... some dollars into euros, please?
10 We're ready to leave, so we'd like to .... now.

52.3 Answer these questions about staying in a hotel.

10 marks

Example: What do you call the evening meal?   *dinner*

1 What do you have to pay before you leave the hotel?
2 What do you probably need if your room is on the ninth floor?
3 What do you need to open your door?
4 What do you call a room for one person?
5 What do you call a room for two people?
6 If you phone Britain from another country, you must always dial 44 before the telephone number. What is the number 44 called?
7 What do you ask for if you want to wake up early in the morning?
8 Complete this sentence: 'I have a .... for a double room.' (The sentence means 'I have booked a double room.')
9 Where do you go when you first arrive at a hotel?
10 What do you need to make a hot drink in your room?

Your score

/30

53.1

6 marks

Where would you hear these phrases? Match the phrases on the left with the places on the right.

1 A cheese sandwich to take away, please.
2 A pint of Shoppam's beer, please.
3 Soup to start, then the chicken and mushrooms, please.
4 A burger, French fries and a coke, please.
5 One coffee, one tea and two pieces of toast, please.
6 Where can I find knives and forks, please?

a café
b fast food restaurant
c self-service restaurant
d sandwich bar
e pub/bar
f restaurant

53.2

20 marks

Fill the gaps.

1 At lunchtime I usually don't have a big meal; I just have a .... , for example a sandwich or some fruit.
2 If you order steak in a restaurant you can usually say if you want it .... , ... or well-..................................... .
3 You don't have to have alcohol in a pub. They also have .... drinks like lemonade or coke.
4 If you want wine with your meal, you can ask the waiter for the wine ....
5 The restaurant has a tourist menu for only €20. You can choose from a list of .... , main courses and .... You can even have a .... meal if you don't eat meat.
6   WAITER: Are you ready to .... , madam?
    CUSTOMER: Yes. I'll have tomato salad to start, then the fish, please.

53.3

4 marks

Put the words into pairs. Use each word once only.

| beef | ~~soup~~ | plain | mashed | ~~tomato~~ | roast |
| gateau | omelette | potatoes | chocolate | | |

Example: tomato soup

1 ....
2 ....
3 ....
4 ....

Your score
/30

54.1 Which sports are these people doing? Write sentences, using either *play* or *go*.

10 marks   *Example:* They are playing football.

1 ....

2 ....

3 ....

4 ....

5 ....

6 ....

7 ....

8 ....

9 ....

10 ....

54.2 Answer these questions.

10 marks
1 If the sea is too cold, where can you go swimming?
2 What do you call the place where you play football?
3 What do you call the place where you play basketball?
4 Name a sport which needs snow.
5 What is another name for *soccer*?
6 Name two sports which originally come from Japan. (*2 marks*)
7 Which sport has the Melbourne Cup?
8 Name one sport in which you can play 'doubles' (two players against two players).
9 Which sport has Formula One?

54.3 Which word does not belong in each group? Explain why.

10 marks
Example: soccer, cricket, table tennis, rugby
         Table tennis – because the others are all played on a field or pitch.

1 swimming, skiing, sailing, canoeing
2 running, motor racing, horse racing, sailing
3 tennis, volleyball, badminton, baseball
4 basketball, table tennis, rugby, cricket
5 tennis, volleyball, basketball, American football

Your score
/30

55 Cinema

55.1

10 marks

Write the names of the types of films next to the pictures. One of the types has two names.

crime	cartoon	musical	love story	detective
comedy	action	horror	science fiction	western

1 ....

2 ....

3 ....

4 ....

5 ....

6 ....

7 ....

(2 marks)

8 ....

9 ....

55.2

12 marks

Correct the mistakes.

1 What's on the cinema this week?
2 At the weekends, we just relax and look videos.
3 I didn't like that film. I was boring.
4 Do you go to cinema very often?
5 It was a very funny film and I enjoyed very much.
6 I watched a good film in TV last night.

55.3

8 marks

Match the words and phrases below with one of the film types from 55.1.

1 'You are a British spy, Mr Bond!'
2 Donald Duck and Mickey Mouse
3 space rockets, men from Mars
4 These films make you laugh a lot.
5 'I love you; I've always loved you!'
6 Dracula, Frankenstein
7 guns, horses, men in big hats, North America
8 Sherlock Holmes, police, murder

Your score

/ 30

56 Leisure at home

56.1
10 marks

Are these statements true or false? If they are false, correct them.

Example: The dog is having a sleep.   False – The dog is listening to the radio.

1 The fair-haired woman is reading a newspaper.
2 The girl is talking on the phone.
3 The man with the beard is watching the news on TV.
4 The dark-haired woman is cooking.
5 The man without a beard is reading a magazine.
6 The boy is playing a computer game.

56.2
10 marks

Choose verbs from the box to complete the conversation.

cook	grown	had	invite	~~playing~~	ring
see	stay	talk	use	watch	

PAUL: Stop ..playing................ computer games, Anna. I want to talk to you. Let's
    (1)........................... Sue and James round at the weekend.
ANNA: Good idea. It's a long time since we (2)........................... friends for dinner. I'll
    (3)........................... them now and ask them. Let's (4)........................... something
    special. They always make such delicious meals.
PAUL: Sure. Let's use some of the vegetables we've (5)........................... in the garden.
ANNA: Good idea. Do you want to (6)........................... the match on TV tonight?
PAUL: No, I'd like to (7)........................... the film on the other channel. What are you going
    to do?
ANNA: I want to (8)........................... to my mother on the phone. I'd like to find out when she
    is going to come and (9)........................... with us. Then I need to (10)...........................
    the Internet to find some information for work.

56.3
10 marks

Use the words below to make sentences.

Example: newspaper / a / day / I / every / read
        I read a newspaper every day.

1 lunch / a / Grandfather / after / always / sleep / has
2 famous / reading / I / people / about / like / books
3 listen / I / the / my / car / radio / usually / in / to
4 films / favourite / musicals / My / are
5 house / a / has / My / plants / of / lot / mother

57 Crime

57.1 Fill the shaded boxes in the chart.

10 marks

Crime	murder	mugging	3	car theft
Person	*Example:* murderer	mugger	terrorist	4 ....
Action	1 to .... somebody	2 to .... somebody	to attack somebody or a place for political reasons	5 to .... a car
Crime	6	shoplifting	9	drug pushing/ dealing
Person	7	8	burglar	10 drug .... / ....
Action	to rob somebody or a place (e.g. a bank)	to steal things from a shop	to break into a house/flat	to sell drugs

57.2 Now use words from 57.1 to fill the gaps in these sentences.

12 marks

1 There was a .... in our street last night. Somebody .... into a house and .... a TV set, a DVD player and some cash.
2 Anna Frane's dead body was found in the river. She had been .... The .... was her ex-boyfriend.
3 .... is very easy in some shops, but many big stores have cameras to catch ....
4 The bank in the High Street was .... yesterday. The .... escaped in a blue sports car.
5 A student was .... as she was walking home. A young man took her money and credit cards.
6 A car .... took my car from the office car park. There have been three .... there this month.

57.3 Answer the questions.

8 marks

1 What word means the opposite of *guilty*?
2 If you do something wrong (e.g. park your car in a 'no parking' area) you have to pay some money. What is this money called?
3 Sometimes people break and destroy things (e.g. telephone boxes, trees in the park). What do we call this crime? What do we call the people who do this crime?
4 Which verb means that the police come and take somebody away because they think they are guilty of a crime?
5 What do we call violence and criminal actions at football matches?
6 What do we call the place where people decide whether someone is guilty of a crime?
7 What do we call the place you have to stay in for many years if you are guilty of a bad crime?

Your score

/30

The media

58.1

Match the words on the left with the definitions on the right.

1 news
2 soap
3 nature programme
4 sports programme
5 talk show
6 cartoon
7 documentary
8 film
9 channel
10 satellite TV
11 comic

a *The Simpsons* and *Mickey Mouse* are famous examples of this
b you can watch this at the cinema or on video
c regular programme about what is happening in the world
d programme which has interviews with famous people
e programme about animals or plants
f programme about, for example, football or the Olympic Games
g CNN, Eurosport, MTV and BBC1 are examples of this
h TV programmes that come via space
i magazine telling stories in pictures
j serious programme about society or nature
k TV serial that goes on for years about the lives of a group of people

58.2

Complete the crossword.

Example: 1 Our new ..*satellite dish*.. lets us get a lot more channels.

2 Mum's new .... has a great article on fashion.
3 She wants to be a .... and write articles for sports magazines.
4 When Pat won the tennis match he had to give an .... to the local paper.
5 The .... took notes during the football match and wrote his article later.
6 I like that .... – there are always interesting guests on it.
7 Buy the children a .... when you are at the newsagent's.
8 I mainly use my .... for word processing.
9 E-mail is one of the most important uses of the ....
10 Mum always watches her favourite Australian .... before the news.
11 This programme is boring. Let's try another ....

58.3

Which of these words go together with *newspaper* and which go together with *magazine*?

Example: news magazine

| women's | computer | news | evening | teenage | morning |

Everyday problems

59.1

10 marks

Look at these pictures and choose a phrase to describe each one.

| It's not working. | It's dying. | He's cut his finger. | It's untidy. | It's broken. |

1 ....

4 ....

2 ....

5 ....

3 ....

59.2

10 marks

What could you do about the problems in 59.1?

1 What could you do to the man's finger?
2 What could you do to the chair or the T.V.? (*2 different verbs*)
3 What could you do to the desk?
4 What could you do to the plant?

59.3

10 marks

Fill the gaps. Use one word in each gap.

1 My computer .... yesterday so I didn't get your e-mail.
2 Our teacher was in a bad .... this morning, so the lesson was not very nice.
3 The ticket machine was out of .... , so I couldn't get a ticket.
4 I shouted at my sister. I must .... to her.
5 Jon and Sara have had a .... and are not speaking to each other.
6 I've .... my wallet. I must find it.
7 I can't find my credit card. Could you help me .... it?
8 The boss doesn't like it if my desk is .... and always asks me to .... it.
9 There's a problem with my bike. Do you think you could .... it for me?

Your score

/30

60.1 Look at the headlines. Which of the problems in the box will these articles be about?

10 marks

| car crash | earthquake | flood | forest fire | hurricane | pollution |
| snowstorm | strike | traffic jam | unemployment | ~~war~~ | |

Example: **BOMBS DESTROY ENEMY TANKS**   *war*

1 **WORKERS STOP WORKING AT CAR FACTORY**

6 **HOUSES UNDER WATER**

7 **FISH DIE IN DIRTY RIVER**

2 **CARS CANNOT MOVE IN CENTRAL LONDON**

8 **ACCIDENT ON MOTORWAY**

3 **STRONG WINDS DESTROY TOWN**

4 *HEAVY SNOW STOPS TRAINS*

9 **MORE PEOPLE WITHOUT JOBS**

5 **MORE TREES BURN IN AUSTRALIA**

10 **BUILDINGS FALL IN CALIFORNIA QUAKE**

60.2 Which word fills each gap?

10 marks

Example: The traffic j _ _ _ are very bad here in the mornings.   *jams*

1 P _ _ _ people don't have much money.
2 U _ _ _ _ _ _ _ _ _ people don't have jobs.
3 H _ _ _ _ _ _ _ people don't have a place to live.
4 If the air is p _ _ _ _ _ _ _ , it is not clean.
5 If people are h _ _ _ _ _ , they want something to eat.
6 The busy time for traffic in the morning and evening is called the r _ _ _ h _ _ _ .
7 The river f _ _ _ _ _ _ last year after some very heavy rain.
8 The manager wouldn't agree to raise the workers' wages and so they decided to go
   o _ s _ _ _ _ _ _ .
9 When the summer is very hot and dry, trees sometimes c _ _ _ _ f _ _ _ .
10 The American W _ _ _ _ I _ _ _ _ _ _ _ _ _ _ _ took place at the end of the eighteenth
   century.

60.3 Put the words in the box in pairs.

10 marks

Example: heavy rain

air	car	cities	crash	crowded	earth
fire	forest	~~heavy~~	homeless	hour	jam
people	pollution	quake	~~rain~~	rush	snow
storm	strong	traffic	wind		

Answer key

Notes on the Answer key and marking scheme.

1 Each test has a total of 30 marks.

2 There is one mark for each correct answer in most exercises. Sometimes there is half ($\frac{1}{2}$) a mark or two marks for each correct answer. You will find the total marks for each exercise below the exercise number on the test page, and on the right hand side in the answer key.

3 If two answers are given in the key (separated by a slash /), both answers are correct (e.g. 'They're having lunch/dinner').

4 Where the answer to one of the questions is given in the text as an example, it appears in brackets – [...] – in the answer key.

Test 1

1.1   1 paragraph   3 dialogue   5 noun   7 sentence   9 phrase
        2 adverb   4 singular   6 adjective   8 preposition   10 plural   (10 marks)

1.2   1 Correct   2 gaps   3 Match   4 Add   5 Complete   (10 marks)

1.3   1 boys (*boy's* means 'something the boy has', for example *the boy's camera*)
        2 adjective (the adverb is *nicely*)
        3 works
        4 man
        5 door   (5 marks)

1.4   1 c   2 e   [3 a]   4 f   5 b   6 d   (5 marks)

Test 2

2.1   1 at   3 tall   5 make   7 have   9 girl
        2 on   4 do   6 have   8 sunny   10 drive   (10 marks)

2.2

[Colours]	Family	Transport	Drink(s)
[black]	father	car	tea
red	brother	bike	coffee
blue	son	bus	juice
green	daughter	train	milk
	mother	motorbike	

(10 marks: half a mark for putting each word in the right family and half a mark for giving each family an appropriate name)

2.3   1 j   2 d   3 h   4 a   5 b   6 k   7 c   8 f   9 e   10 i   (10 marks)

Test 3

3.1   1 He's having a shower.
        2 They're / The students are having a lesson.
        3 She's having a cup of coffee. / She's having (a) coffee.
        4 They're having a party.
        5 They're having lunch/dinner / a meal / something to eat.   (5 marks)

3.2   1 d   2 c   3 a   4 e   5 b   (5 marks)

3.3   1 hadn't / had not got / didn't have; had to   4 has to; have got; have to
         2 had   5 have
         3 Have … got; have   6 had   (10 marks)

3.4   *Possible answers*:
         1 Bye-bye! Have a good/safe flight/journey/trip!   4 Bye! Have a good time/evening!
         2 Wow! Can I have a go?   5 Can I have a word (with you)?
         3 Can I have a look (at them)?   (5 marks)

3.5   1 meal   2 meeting   3 appointment   4 homework; exam   (5 marks)

Test 4

4.1   1 by   3 away   5 up; down   7 back
         2 out of; into/onto   4 up   6 on   8 to   (10 marks)

4.2   1 c   2 a   3 b   4 c   5 b   (5 marks)

4.3   1 Nora is going shopping.   4 Terry and Sarah are going sightseeing.
         2 Harry is going swimming.   5 Nick is going fishing.
         3 Mel and Bob are going dancing.   (5 marks)

4.4   On Monday evening Jim is going to meet Tom and Ricky.
         On Tuesday he is going to visit his grandmother.
         On Wednesday he is going to meet Pat for dinner.
         On Thursday morning he is going to have his hair cut.
         On Thursday evening he is going to play table tennis with Mary.
         On Friday he is going to write a report for work.
         On Friday he is also going to phone his Aunt Sally.
         On Saturday he is going to buy Tom a birthday present.
         On Sunday he is going to give Tom his present.
         On Sunday he is also going to take Mary to Tom's party.   (10 marks)

Test 5

5.1   1 done; did   2 Does; doesn't; does   3 Did; did; didn't   4 do; done   (10 marks)

5.2   1 What do you do?
         2 What do you do at the weekends?
         3 Let me do the washing-up / let me do the dishes.
         4 I always do the/my housework on Saturdays.
         5 I did my best / a lot of work but I failed the exam.   (5 marks)

5.3   1 MICHAEL: What *does* your father *do*?
                 JANE: He's a lorry-driver.
         2 I don't like *doing* homework but I know I have to *do it*.
         3 He *does* a lot of business with companies in the USA nowadays.
         4 I saw her at the gym. She *was doing* some exercises that looked very hard.
         5 DIANA: Liz, what *are you doing* with all those clothes?
                  LIZ: *I'm doing* my washing. All my clothes are dirty.
         6 FATHER: Ivan, *do* your homework now!
                  IVAN: No. Not now. *I'll do* it later. Please Dad!
                FATHER: No! I want you *to do* it now!

7 MARIA: I *do* my best to learn all the new words every day.
ANONA: So *do* I, but then I forget them again.
8 In our family, my father *does* the washing-up every day, my mother *does* the gardening, but my brother never *does* anything! (15 marks)

Test 6

6.1 1 Pam is making (some / a cup of) tea.
2 Tim is making a photocopy.
3 Rose is making a cake.
4 Chris is making a video/film.
5 Isabelle is making a dress.
6 Phil is making an appointment (with the dentist).
7 Sophie is making a mistake.
8 Vincent is making dinner/lunch / a meal.
9 Katy is making a/her/the bed.
10 Nathan is making (some / a cup of) coffee. (10 marks)

6.2 do: your homework, some exercises, your best, the cooking, the dishes, the housework
make: [lunch], a noise, an appointment, a mistake, a decision (10 marks)

6.3 I did it very quickly so I think I probably *made* a lot of mistakes. Then my friend and I went to a film. The hero died so it made us feel very *sad/unhappy*. After the film we went to a café. The food smelt very good, which made me feel very *hungry*. The food wasn't very good, but at least I didn't have to *do* the dishes.
I've got to *take/do* an exam next week, but let's meet at the weekend.

(10 marks:
1 for identifying each mistake and 1 for each correction)

Test 7

7.1 1 coming home   4 comes from
2 come here   5 I'll come back
3 coming out of   (5 marks)

7.2 1 c   2 e   3 a   4 b   5 d   (5 marks)

7.3 1 LORNA: Has your brother come back *from* Germany yet?
JAMES: Yes, he *came home* last Friday.
2 HILDA: Do you know Stockholm? I've never been there.
RYAN: Yes, I *went* there last summer for a few days.
3 STEVE: What nationality is Tanya? Where *does she come* from?
FELIX: She *comes from* Moscow. She's Russian.
4 ANNA: I was surprised to see Julia in your office.
NANCY: Yes, she didn't even knock. She just came *in*.
5 EVA: Do you know what the English word 'cabbage' means?
PACO: Yes, it *came up* in the lesson yesterday. It's a vegetable.
6 ADA: Would you like to *come* round to my house this evening to watch a video?
NIK: Yes, but my cousin is staying with me. Can he come *along*?
ADA: Of course. He can *come* too.

(20 marks:
2 for each corrected mistake)

Test 8

8.1
1 It took Miranda an/one hour to go/get to work.
2 It took Tony twenty minutes to check his e-mails.
3 It took Maggie an hour and a quarter / an hour and fifteen minutes to do her homework.
4 It took Jeremy an hour and a half / an hour and thirty minutes / ninety minutes to fly/get to Paris.
5 It took Julia ten minutes to eat (her) lunch.
6 It took Mark two and a half hours to write the report.
7 It took Angela three hours forty minutes to go/get to London.
8 It took Paul three and a half hours to repair his bike.
9 It took Rosemary three months to write a/her story.
10 It took Ken seven years to write a/his poem.   (10 marks)

8.2
1 I took the train when I went to the airport last summer.
2 Anita is taking an English exam tomorrow. / Anita is going to take an English exam tomorrow.
3 Kay wants to take (some) Greek lessons.
4 Her father takes/took the bus to the office.
5 Pete took his driving test yesterday.   (10 marks: 2 for each sentence.
                    Give yourself 1 mark if you have just one mistake in the sentence.)

8.3
a scarf   b money   c [umbrella]   d camera   e book   f apple
1 book   2 apple   3 camera   4 money   5 scarf   (10 marks:
                    1 for labelling each picture, 1 for completing each sentence)

Test 9

9.1
1 brings   2 taking   3 brought   4 bring   5 Take
                                                                                (10 marks:
                    1 for each correct choice of *take* or *bring*, 1 for each correct verb form)

9.2
These are suggested answers. Yours may be a little different, but you must choose the correct verb, *take* or *bring*, to get the marks.
1 I'll take / I can take / Let me take you to the station. / Do you want me to take you to the station?*
   *If you are learning English in Ireland you may hear people saying *bring* here instead of *take*.
2 Will/would/can/could you take this parcel to the post office for me, please?
3 Would you like to come to our/my party and bring your guitar?
4 I'm going to take it back and change it / get a different size / get the right size.
5 Will/would/can/could you bring me back some Belgian chocolates?   (10 marks)

9.3

Tuesday 4 March 2003
Hi Ellen, Guess what? Tim *took* me to the cinema last night and today when I was studying at home he came to see me and *brought* me some flowers! I think he must be in love with me! Bye, Marian

(10 marks: 2 for each corrected mistake)

Test 10

10.1

1 warm(er)	5 thin(ner)/slim(mer)	9 cards/presents
2 interesting/exciting	6 ticket	10 e-mails/messages
3 shorter	7 money/cash	
4 rich(er)	8 bread/cakes	(10 marks)

10.2
1 How do I get to the (railway/train) station?
2 How do I get to the theatre?
3 How do I get to the cinema?
4 How do I get to the bank?
5 How do I get to the restaurant? (10 marks: 1 for writing
How do I get to correctly and 1 for the correct place)

10.3

1 are getting	3 get	5 is getting	7 get	9 to get
2 got	4 gets	6 to get	8 got	10 getting (10 marks)

Test 11

11.1

1 on	3 up	5 over	7 take	9 put
2 turn	4 do	6 turn/switch	8 off	10 on (10 marks)

11.2 1 d   2 c   3 e   4 a   5 b (10 marks)

11.3
1 get *on* very well with him   4 she turned it *down*
2 I went *on* working   5 I've got *over* it
3 put *on* your raincoat (10 marks)

Test 12

12.1
1 gets up   4 goes to work
2 goes to the bathroom   5 gets to the office
3 has breakfast (5 marks)

12.2 1 comes home   4 cleans his teeth
      2 makes dinner   5 goes to bed
      3 has dinner   (5 marks)

12.3 1 Andy is watching TV.   6 Andy is going to bed.
      2 Andy is having (his) breakfast.   7 Andy is having dinner / eating.
      3 Andy is making dinner / cooking.   8 Andy is going to/coming home from work.
      4 Andy is getting up.   9 Andy is coming/arriving home.
      5 Andy is phoning/calling a friend.   10 Andy is waking up.   (10 marks)

12.4 1 What time do you go to work?   6 What time do you (usually) go to bed?
      2 How often do you clean the house?   7 How often do you go to the supermarket?
      3 What time do you (normally) get up?   8 What time do you (usually) come home?
      4 How often do you go for a walk?   9 How often do you go to your friend's house?
      5 How often do you wash your clothes?   10 How often do you write letters?
                                                                    (10 marks)

Test 13

13.1 1 b   2 a   3 d   4 e   5 c   (5 marks)
      (Note: 1c, 1e, 4b, 4c are also possible.)

13.2 1 say   2 told   3 say   4 tell   5 tell   (5 marks)

13.3 *Possible answers:*
      1 Ask somebody the way. / Ask somebody how to get there. / Ask for directions.
      2 Ask somebody the time. / Ask somebody what the time is. / Ask somebody what
         time it is. / Ask somebody if they have (got) the time.
      3 Ask the teacher (to explain it). / Ask another student to help you. / Ask for a dictionary.
      4 Ask (the waiter) for the bill.
      5 Ask them to turn it down / turn it off.   (10 marks)

13.4 1 Will you *answer* it
      2 she *speaks* excellent Danish
      3 he hasn't *replied (to it)* / *answered it* yet
      4 How *do you say* 'Milan' in Italian?
      5 He *told* me an interesting story   (10 marks)

Test 14

14.1 1 He's driving a bus.   6 He's swimming.
      2 He's riding a horse.   7 She's dancing.
      3 She's walking.   8 He's flying.
      4 She's falling.   9 He's climbing a tree.
      5 She's jumping.   10 He's carrying a door.   (10 marks)

14.2 1 b   2 c   3 a   4 b   5 b   6 c   7 b   8 c   9 a   10 c   (10 marks)

14.3 1 running; swimming; riding   4 jogs
      2 drive; fly   5 walk; carry
      3 dancing   6 falling   (10 marks)

Test 15

15.1
1 Before; because 5 After (*When* or *Before* would also be possible here.)
2 If; and   6 so
3 even   7 when
4 also; but   (10 marks)

15.2 1 b   2 c   3 a   4 c   5 b   (10 marks)

15.3
I'm going to study abroad though I can't speak any foreign languages.
I'm going to study abroad so I will be away from home for three years.
I'm going to study abroad when I've finished secondary school.
I'm going to study abroad if I get good grades in my exams.
I'm going to study abroad because I want to learn more about other countries and cultures.
                                                                  (10 marks)

Test 16

16.1
1 June   3 August   5 July   7 February   9 April
2 December   4 January   6 October   8 September   10 November (10 marks)

16.2 1 f   2 k   [3 g]   4 h   5 j   6 d   7 i   8 e   9 b   10 c   11 a   (10 marks)

16.3
1 after   4 in; in
2 in; in   5 before
3 at; on; on   6 in   (10 marks)

Test 17

17.1
1 o'clock
2 hours ago
3 for two hours / since two o'clock   (5 marks)

17.2
1 May   4 Bill is on holiday for two weeks.
2 March   5 April 23rd
3 February   (5 marks)

17.3

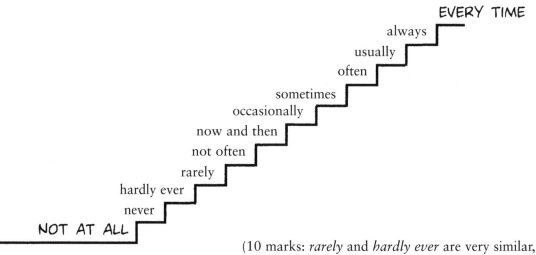

(10 marks: *rarely* and *hardly ever* are very similar,
so give yourself the marks if you have *hardly ever* before *rarely*.
The same is true for *occasionally* and *now and then*.)

17.4
1 never; always
2 now and then; often
3 hardly ever; usually
4 not often; occasionally
5 Usually; sometimes

(5 marks)

17.5
1 At; moment; twice
2 in a; soon
3 once; recently
4 the past
5 the future

(5 marks)

Test 18

18.1
back – front
beginning – end
bottom – top
here – there
left – right

(10 marks)

18.2
| 1 a dog | 3 the number 1 | 5 a woman | 7 a hat | 9 a boy |
| 2 a flag | 4 a cat | 6 a book | 8 a tree | 10 a house |

(10 marks)

18.3
| 1 here | 3 away | 5 middle | 7 there | 9 everywhere |
| 2 out | 4 abroad | 6 back | 8 left | 10 side |

(10 marks)

Test 19

19.1

Opposites	
good	bad
fast	slow
quiet	loud
sad	happy
friendly	unfriendly

(10 marks)

19.2
1 fast
2 loudly
3 quietly
4 well
5 slowly
6 in a very unfriendly way
7 badly
8 happily
9 sadly
10 in a friendly way

(10 marks)

19.3
1 Harry/He spoke impolitely (to his teacher).
2 Glen/He was acting strangely.
3 The accident happened suddenly.
4 Pippa/She passed it / the exam easily.
5 He finished the job quickly.

(10 marks)

Test 20

20.1
| 1 threw | 3 flew | 5 shone | 7 met | 9 shut |
| 2 drank | 4 swam | 6 broke | 8 spent | 10 chose |

(10 marks)

20.2

Infinitive	Past simple	Past participle
cut	[cut]	[cut]
catch	caught	**caught**
forget	**forgot**	forgotten
write	**wrote**	**written**
become	became	**become**
ride	**rode**	ridden
shoot	**shot**	**shot**
steal	stole	**stolen**
begin	**began**	begun
feel	**felt**	**felt**
stand	stood	**stood**

(10 marks: ½ each)

20.3
1 caught
2 cut
3 wrote; began
4 stole; shot
5 become
6 rode; stood
7 forgotten

(10 marks)

Test 21

21.1
1 information
2 accommodation
3 weather
4 furniture
5 luggage

(10 marks)

21.2

Countable	Uncountable
shoe	rice
plate	milk
apple	money
bus	bread
	butter
	traffic

(10 marks)

21.3
1 *Is this furniture* new? I haven't seen *it* before. (2 marks)
2 gave us *advice* (or gave us *some advice*)
3 three large *loaves of bread*
4 *some* sugar
5 The *traffic is* always very bad
6 The news *is* on TV in five minutes. Shall we watch *it*? (2 marks)
7 Rail *travel* is more interesting
8 a lot of *work*

(10 marks)

Test 22

22.1

Good	Bad
best	dreadful
better	ghastly
brilliant	horrendous
excellent	horrible
fine	terrible
gorgeous	worse
great	worst
lovely	
marvellous	
nice	
perfect	
superb	
wonderful	

(10 marks: ½ each)

22.2
1 great	3 excellent	5 brilliant	7 perfect	9 fine
2 horrible	4 awful	6 lovely	8 best	10 horrendous

(10 marks)

22.3
1 Perfect	5 marvellous	9 superb
2 ghastly	6 Excellent	10 dreadful
3 Lovely	7 awful	
4 horrible/horrendous	8 Wonderful	

(10 marks)

Test 23

23.1

Adjective	+ or −	Adjective	+ or −
stupid	−	lovely	+
easy-going	+	happy	+
selfish	−	horrible	−
kind	+	nice	+
difficult	−	intelligent	+

(10 marks)

23.2
1 happy	3 easy-going	5 nice	7 intelligent	9 difficult
2 selfish	4 horrible	6 kind	8 stupid	10 lovely

(10 marks)

23.3
1 well-behaved	4 to
2 naughty/badly-behaved	5 of
3 intelligent/clever	

(10 marks)

Test 24

24.1 [1 f]   2 i   3 k   4 a   5 g   6 b   7 j   8 e   9 c   10 d   11 h   (10 marks)

24.2
1 for	4 about (*of* is also possible)	7 for
2 to	5 at; at	8 at
3 of	6 to	9 to

(10 marks)

24.3
1 apologise	3 wait	5 pay	7 used	9 afraid
2 good	4 listen	6 proud	8 belong	10 look (10 marks)

Test 25

25.1
1 pre-war	4 resend	7 uncomfortable	10 unfinished
2 non-smoking	5 ex-girlfriend	8 retell	
3 half-price	6 unhappy	9 informal	(10 marks)

25.2
1 He is the *ex-president* of the club.
2 I like *non-alcoholic* wine.
3 I think you should *rewrite* your essay.
4 He seems to be *unhappy* in his job.
5 The restaurant has *half-price* meals for children.
6 I don't like to give *unfinished* homework to my teacher.
7 The *pre-school* years are very important for little children.
8 It is *impossible* for anyone to live for 200 years.
9 You can wear *informal* clothes to the party.
10 This chair is *uncomfortable*. (10 marks)

25.3
1 This machine is *unsafe*.	6 The lessons are very *informal*
2 something *incorrect*	7 Mike is my *ex-boss*.
3 She is very *impolite*	8 smoking or *non-smoking* seat
4 *pre-exam* nerves	9 a *half-hour* drive
5 some *unread* books	10 I *readdressed* the letter (10 marks)

Test 26

26.1

Suffix	Meaning of suffix	Example
1 er, or	person	footballer, swimmer, actor
2 er, or	machine or thing	tin opener, pencil sharpener
3 ology	subject of study	psychology, geology
4 less	without	endless, sleepless
5 ness	makes an abstract noun from an adjective	sadness, weakness

(10 marks: 1 for each suffix and 1 for adding another example.
Check in a dictionary if you are not sure whether the example
you suggest is correct or not.)

26.2
1 Mike swims strongly.	4 Paula dances beautifully.
2 Jim walks slowly.	5 That footballer plays wonderfully.
3 The children work happily.	

(10 marks: 1 for the correct verb
and 1 for the correct adverb)

26.3
1 politics – e	4 economics – d
2 sunny – c	5 rainy – f
3 sandy – b	

(10 marks: 1 for forming the correct word and
1 for matching the phrase to the right picture)

Test 27

27.1 1 b 2 b 3 a 4 b 5 b 6 a 7 a 8 b 9 b 10 b (10 marks)

27.2

Word	Same sound
1 quiet	diet
2 lose	shoes
3 quite	fight
4 felt	belt
5 loose	juice

(10 marks)

27.3
1 I *lent* her my pen
2 a really good *cook*
3 I *fell* down the stairs
4 *expecting* to fail
5 *borrow* your tennis racket
6 They *check* your age
7 said '*Good afternoon*' (Note: You say 'Good evening' when you arrive at someone's house between 5 pm and about 8 pm. If you arrive between 12 pm and 5 pm you say 'Good afternoon'. You say 'Good night' when you <u>leave</u> someone's house (after about 9 pm).)
8 I *did* some shopping
9 Can you *tell* me
10 *speak* Spanish

(10 marks)

Test 28

28.1 1 were 3 honeymoon 5 died 7 call; after
        2 got; to 4 married 6 of 8 ill (10 marks)

28.2 1 widowed 2 married 3 divorced 4 single (4 marks)

28.3
1 They are getting married.
2 A wedding.
3 The bride.
4 The (bride)groom.
5 The honeymoon.
6 marriage

(6 marks)

28.4
1 How much does/did he weigh?; What are they going to call him? / What are they calling him?
2 What did he die of?
3 What did the bride wear?; Where did they go on/for (their) honeymoon? (10 marks: 2 each)

Test 29

29.1
1 my daughter
2 my uncle
3 my son
4 his sister/brother
5 my father
6 my grandmother
7 my grandson
8 my grandfather
9 my aunt
10 my grandparents

(10 marks)

29.2 **Across**
1 daughter
2 cousin
3 parents

Down
4 uncle
5 sister
6 nieces (12 marks)

29.3 1 NO (My *uncle* John is my mother's sister's husband. / My nephew John is *my sister's/brothers son*.)
2 YES
3 NO (Mary is David's *wife*. / David is Mary's husband.)
4 YES (8 marks)

Test 30

30.1
1 shoulder	5 knee	9 mouth
2 stomach	6 neck	10 leg
3 finger	7 heart	
4 thumb	8 nose	

A	T	M	T	O	O	T	H
S	H	O	U	L	D	E	R
T	U	U	N	E	C	K	F
O	M	T	N	M	O	M	I
M	B	H	O	P	A	R	N
A	G	E	S	A	L	E	G
C	A	R	E	K	N	E	E
H	E	A	R	T	I	P	R

(10 marks: ½ for labelling each picture and ½ for each word found)

30.2
1 eyes; ears	4 blood	7 thumb
2 hair; nails	5 brain	8 back; side; front
3 bust; waist; hips	6 skin	9 like 'ch' in *chemist*

(14 marks)

30.3
1 Her *hair is* black.	4 Please wash *your* hands
2 a pain in *his* side	5 My *feet* hurt. (*or* My *foot hurts*.)
3 two *teeth*	6 put *their* hands up

(6 marks)

Test 31

31.1
1 socks	3 shirt	5 boots	7 coat	9 hat
2 belt	4 tie	6 skirt	8 scarf	10 gloves

(10 marks)

31.2 1 why 2 run 3 note 4 shoot 5 half (5 marks)

31.3 trousers   tights   jeans   shorts   sunglasses (5 marks)

31.4 1 when you get up   6 a suit
       2 a ring   7 jumper
       3 on your head   8 Robert is carrying an umbrella.
       4 sunglasses   9 Lisa has put a skirt on.
       5 a woman   10 At night, I *get undressed* and go to bed.   (10 marks)

Test 32

32.1

Eyes	Skin	Hair	Height and weight
dark	dark	dark	fat
green	fair	fair	short
brown		brown	slim
		short	tall
		long	thin*

* We can also talk about 'thin hair' if someone does not have very much hair.
(10 marks: ½ if you do not put the word in all the possible columns)

32.2 1 Sasha is slim.   4 Tamara is pretty.
       2 My boss is elderly.   5 Pat is overweight.
       3 My brother is handsome.   (5 marks)

32.3 1 No, she's got *short, dark* hair. (2 marks)
       2 No, she's *tall* and *thin/slim*. (2 marks)
       3 No, it's *old/elderly*.
       4 No, he's *handsome*.
       5 No, she's got *dark/black/brown* hair.
       6 No, he's *fat/overweight*.
       7 No, she's *ordinary-looking/ugly*.
       8 No, he/she's *short*.   (10 marks)

32.4 1 He's got a beard/moustache.   4 He's got short/dark/brown/black hair.
       2 He's also got a moustache/beard.   5 He is handsome/young.
       3 His skin is dark.   (5 marks)
(Note: other answers are possible. Give yourself a mark for each correct answer.)

Test 33

33.1 1 d   2 e   3 a   4 b   5 c   (10 marks)

33.2 1 headache   2 malaria   3 asthma   4 cancer   5 cholera   (5 marks)

33.3 1 cholera   2 asthma   3 cancer   4 headache   5 malaria   (5 marks)

33.4 1 stress; relax   5 Exercise
       2 attack; hospital   6 cold
       3 hay-fever; sneeze   7 aspirin
       4 diet   (10 marks)

Test 34

34.1 1 You feel hungry.   5 You feel ill.   9 You feel sad.
       2 You feel tired.   6 You feel cold.   10 You feel surprised.
       3 You feel angry.   7 You feel happy.
       4 You feel thirsty.   8 You feel hot.   (10 marks)

34.2 1 dislike   2 hate   3 hot   4 sad/unhappy   5 well   (5 marks)

34.3 1 I dislike abstract paintings.
2 I want my brother to get a new job.
3 Jack hopes (that) his girlfriend phones / will phone (him) soon.
4 I prefer strawberry ice cream to vanilla ice cream.
5 My little sister likes juice more than milk.   (5 marks)

34.4 1 The tall girl looks *upset*.
2 The fat man looks *angry*.
3 The old man looks *sad*.
4 The short girl looks *ill*.
5 The thin man looks *surprised*.
6 The boy with dark hair looks *warm*.
7 The boy with fair hair looks *tired*.
8 The woman with long hair looks *happy*.
9 The dog looks *thirsty*.
10 The cat looks *hungry*.   (10 marks)

Test 35

35.1 1 Good *morning*.
2 Good *evening*. (Note: Not 'Goodnight'. You say 'Goodnight' when you leave, not when you arrive.)
3 *Cheers*, everybody!
4 *Excuse me*, please.
5 *Bless you*!   (10 marks)

35.2 RON: *Hello/Hi*, Fiona.
FIONA: *Hi/Hello*, Ron.
RON: *How are you?*
FIONA: Fine. *And you?*
RON: *Not too bad, thanks*. It's my birthday today.
FIONA: Oh! *Happy birthday*!
RON: Thanks. So, how's university?
FIONA: Oh, great. In fact I just passed a big exam.
RON: Oh good! *Congratulations*!
FIONA: Thanks. The only problem is I've got another one next week.
RON: Really? Oh well, *good luck*!
FIONA: Thanks. Well, I must go now. Are you going to Anne's party on Saturday?
RON: Yeah. Well, *see you soon*, then.
FIONA: Yes. *Goodbye*, see you at the party.
RON: Bye.   (10 marks)

35.3 1 LIM: Chinese New Year starts this week.
     DEREK: Oh really? *Happy* New Year!
2 DIANE: Here's the newspaper you asked me to get.
     NORBERT: *Thanks / thank you*.
     DIANE: No problem.
3 RUTH: This is my last day in the office till December 28th.
     WILL: Oh, well, I'll say *Happy/Merry* Christmas, then.
     RUTH: Thanks. You too.

4 GEOFF: I swam a kilometre today.
   FRAN: Well *done*! You must be very fit.
   GEOFF: Yeah, I feel good.
5 BETH: It's my birthday today.
   SONYA: Oh, *happy birthday*!
   BETH: Thank you.   (10 marks)

Test 36

36.1 Argentina, Brazil and Paraguay are in South America.
Canada and the USA are in North America.
Egypt, Ethiopia, Libya and Zimbabwe are in Africa.
Russia is in both Asia and Europe.
Afghanistan, China, Japan, Mongolia and Singapore are in Asia.
Finland, Italy, Germany, Slovakia and Spain are in Europe.   (10 marks: ½ each)

36.2

Country	Adjective	Language
France	[French]	[French]
Holland, the Netherlands	Dutch	Dutch
Iceland	Icelandic	Icelandic
Iraq	Iraqi	Arabic
Korea	Korean	Korean
Norway	Norwegian	Norwegian
Peru	Peruvian	Spanish
Portugal	Portuguese	Portuguese
Saudi Arabia	Saudi (Arabian)	Arabic
Switzerland	Swiss	French, German, Italian, Romansch *
Thailand	Thai	Thai

* Give yourself ½ if you have two or more of these four official Swiss languages.
(10 marks: ½ each)

36.3 1 Ottawa is the capital of Canada.
2 Santiago is the capital of Chile.
3 Athens is the capital of Greece.
4 Budapest is the capital of Hungary.
5 Caracas is the capital of Venezuela.
6 Ankara is the capital of Turkey.
7 Montevideo is the capital of Uruguay.
8 Kathmandu is the capital of Nepal.
9 Stockholm is the capital of Sweden.
10 Damascus is the capital of Syria.   (10 marks: ½ for each sentence)

Test 37

37.1   1 e   2 d   3 b   4 j   5 h   6 c   7 f   8 a   9 i   10 g   (10 marks)

37.2
1 foggy	3 X		5 windy	7 snowy	9 X	
2 sunny	4 thundery	6 X		8 rainy	10 cloudy	(10 marks)

37.3
1 What lovely weather! (*Weather* is uncountable; we cannot say *a weather*.)
2 and *foggy* in Chicago
3 It's very *dry*
4 a *thunderstorm*
5 raining and *windy*   (10 marks)

Test 38

38.1
1 bus stop	3 tourist information office	5 no entry
2 crossroads	4 no parking	(5 marks)

38.2
1 museum	3 library	5 librarian
2 bank	4 policeman / police officer	(5 marks)

38.3
1 railway station	4 traffic warden	7 pedestrian area	10 car park
2 post office	5 shop assistant	8 shopping centre	
3 bank clerk	6 traffic lights	9 town hall	(20 marks)

Test 39

39.1   1 g   2 d   3 h   4 b   5 j   6 a   7 e   8 i   9 c   10 f   (10 marks)

39.2
1 village	3 forests	5 mountains	7 cottage	9 farm
2 path	4 river	6 lake	8 field	10 hills	(10 marks)

39.3
1 I love *nature/wildlife*; a *conservation area* (2 marks)
2 we go *skiing* there / we go there *to* ski
3 a walk in *the country* / *the countryside*
4 There *is* some fantastic *wildlife*
5 in the *mountains*
6 a *city* in the *country* of Greece (2 marks)
7 the highest *mountains*
8 go *for a walk* / go *walking*   (10 marks)

Test 40

40.1
1 snake	3 horse	5 giraffe	7 cow	9 monkey
2 elephant	4 tortoise	6 cat	8 parrot	10 fish	(10 marks)

40.2
1 a foal	6 ham, pork, bacon (1 mark each for any two of these)
2 chicken	7 milk
3 a budgie/budgerigar	8 a snake
4 eggs	9 leather
5 wool	(10 marks)

40.3
1 Horse – because the others are all kinds of cats.
2 Snake – because the others have four legs and are mammals.
3 Sheep – because the others are all young/baby animals.
4 Pig – because the others are all pets. / Fish – because it lives in water and the others live on land.
5 Foal – because the others are all types of meat.
                                            (10 marks: 1 for the word and 1 for the reason.
                          Note: there are other possible answers with different reasons.)

Test 41

41.1
1 bus/coach
2 boat
3 underground
4 (aero)plane
5 motorbike/motorcycle
6 taxi
7 helicopter
8 ship/ferry
9 train
10 bicycle/bike   (10 marks)

41.2
1 a map / atlas
2 your/a passport
3 the buffet/restaurant car
4 a single (ticket) / a one-way ticket
5 the customs / the customs officer
6 luggage
7 a timetable
8 hire one / rent one
9 a boarding card
10 flight stewards / flight attendants / cabin attendants / cabin crew / cabin staff
(10 marks)

41.3   1 c   2 a   3 c   4 b   5 a   (10 marks)

Test 42

42.1
1 You can go out (of) this door.
2 You can pull this door (towards you).
3 The shop is open for business. You can buy things there.
4 You must not walk on the grass.
5 You must queue/wait / stand in line on the side shown.
6 You can buy things more cheaply / for a lower price.
7 The phone is not working. You can't use it.
8 You must pay for your things there / in the place shown.
9 You can ring the bell if you want help.
10 You must not smoke here.   (10 marks)

42.2
1 ENTRANCE / WAY IN
2 PUSH
3 MEN WC / TOILET
4 CLOSED
5 WAY OUT / EXIT   (5 marks)

42.3
1 SALE
2 TOILET; WC
3 PUSH
4 CLOSED
5 NO SMOKING
6 PULL
7 PLEASE RING FOR ATTENTION
8 EXIT; WAY OUT
9 OUT OF ORDER
10 ENTRANCE; WAY IN
11 PLEASE PAY HERE
12 PLEASE QUEUE THIS SIDE   (15 marks)

Test 43

43.1
1 **Down**
  1 onion
  2 grapes

Across
3 oranges
4 banana
5 pear

2 **Across**
  1 pineapple
  2 carrots
  3 tomatoes
  4 beans

Down
5 potatoes   (10 marks)

43.2　　1　Pineapples　　3　tomatoes　　5　potatoes　　7　beans　　9　carrots
　　　　　　2　Onions　　　　4　banana　　　6　Pears　　　8　Oranges　10　grapes　(10 marks)

43.3　　1　fish　　　　　　　　　　　　　4　Strawberries
　　　　　　2　wine; fruit juice　　　　　　5　garlic
　　　　　　3　pizza; hamburgers; hot-dogs　6　pasta; peas　　　　　　　　(10 marks)

Test 44

44.1　　1　saucepan　　3　sink　　　5　cooker　　　7　mug/cup　　9　shelf
　　　　　　2　cupboard　　4　knife　　6　microwave　8　teapot　　　10　frying pan　(10 marks)

44.2　　2　cloth　　　　4　plate　　　6　tap　　　8　saucer　　10　wastebin
　　　　　　3　bowl　　　　5　spoon　　7　fridge　　9　fork

　　　　　　The word in the tinted box is *chopsticks*.　　　　　　　　　　(10 marks)

44.3　　1　help　　2　find　　3　go　　4　put　　5　use　　　　　　　(5 marks)

44.4　　coffee maker　　　　　　　　　　washing-up liquid
　　　　　　kitchen roll　　　　　　　　　　worktop
　　　　　　tea towel　　　　　　　　　　　　　　　　　　　　　　　　(5 marks)

Test 45

45.1　　1　alarm clock　　　5　bed　　　　　　　9　nightdress
　　　　　　2　cupboard　　　　6　bedside lamp　　10　bedside table
　　　　　　3　pyjamas　　　　7　wardrobe
　　　　　　4　chest of drawers　8　dressing table　　　　　　　　　　　(10 marks)

45.2　　1　toothbrush　　　6　bath
　　　　　　2　toothpaste　　　7　toilet
　　　　　　3　soap　　　　　　8　shampoo
　　　　　　4　basin　　　　　9　towel
　　　　　　5　shelf　　　　　10　shower　　　　　　　　　　　　　　(10 marks)

45.3　　Every morning, when my alarm clock *rings* (we often say *goes off* too) I *wake*
　　　　　　up. Then I *get* up and have a shower and *get* dressed. I go downstairs and
　　　　　　have breakfast. Then I go back to the bathroom and *clean* my teeth. At the
　　　　　　end of the day, at about 11.30, I go upstairs, *get* undressed and go *to* bed.
　　　　　　I listen *to* the radio for a while then I turn *off* the light (or *turn the light off*)
　　　　　　and go to *sleep*.　　　　　　　　　　　　　　　　　　　　(10 marks)

Test 46

46.1　　1　armchair, chair, sofa
　　　　　　2　carpet
　　　　　　3　bookshelf, table, coffee table, desk
　　　　　　4　radio, TV, CD player, music centre
　　　　　　5　light, reading lamp, curtains (*light switch* is also possible)
　　　　　　6　remote control
　　　　　　7　light switch
　　　　　　8　book, phone book
　　　　　　9　power point　　　　　　　　　　　　　　(10 marks: ½ each)

46.2

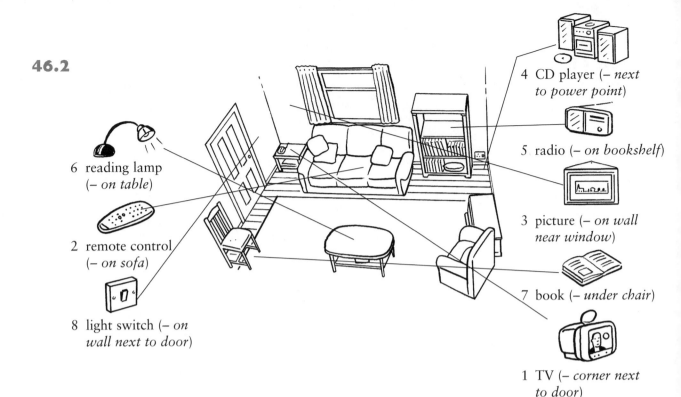

6 reading lamp (– *on table*)

2 remote control (– *on sofa*)

8 light switch (– *on wall next to door*)

4 CD player (– *next to power point*)

5 radio (– *on bookshelf*)

3 picture (– *on wall near window*)

7 book (– *under chair*)

1 TV (– *corner next to door*)

(16 marks: 1 for correct number and 1 for correct line)

46.3   1 close/shut   2 turn /switch; off / turn; down   3 watch   4 relax   (4 marks)

Test 47

47.1
1 a hairdresser
2 a secretary (could also be an *administrative assistant* or (informal) *an admin assistant*)
3 a farmer
4 a doctor
5 an engineer
6 a mechanic
7 a waiter (*waitress* can be used for a woman)
8 a nurse
9 a teacher
10 a shop assistant   (10 marks)

47.2
1 mechanic
2 farmer
3 hairdresser
4 teacher
5 secretary (or *personal assistant* or (informal) *PA* or *administrative assistant*)
6 shop assistant
7 engineer
8 doctor
9 nurses
10 waiters/waitresses
(10 marks)

47.3
1 False: a bus driver drives a bus.
2 True
3 False: a person who drives a taxi is a *taxi-driver*.
4 True (can also be called an *author*)
5 True
6 False: you can say *I have interesting work* or *I have an interesting job*.
7 True
8 False: you would say *I'm a teacher*.
9 False: a person who repairs cars is called a *mechanic*.
10 True
(10 marks)

Test 48

48.1
1 geography
2 art
3 biology
4 physical education / P.E.
5 maths, mathematics
6 history
7 information technology / I.T.
8 physics
9 music
10 chemistry

(10 marks)

48.2
1 OHP – b
2 board – j or f
3 ruler – d
4 notebook – g
5 paper clip – c
6 rubber – i
7 cassette – k
8 drawing pin – e
9 noticeboard – f
10 pencil sharpener – h

(10 marks)

48.3
1 doing
2 giving
3 take
4 learn
5 doing
6 ends/finishes; take/do
7 pass; fail
8 teaches

(10 marks)

Test 49

49.1
1 keyboard
2 letter
3 mobile phone
4 post box
5 telephone
6 screen

(6 marks)

49.2
1 address
2 answerphone
3 box
4 mouse
5 (floppy) disk/CD

(10 marks)

49.3
Hello, seven six three double-eight five.
Hi, can I speak to Ken?
He's not here right now. Who's calling?
It's Joanna. Could you give him a message?
Yeah.
Could you tell him I called and I'll call back later.
Okay, I'll tell him.
Thanks.
No problem. Bye.
Bye.

(10 marks)

49.4
1 What is your fax number?
2 What is your e-mail address?
3 Can I make a (phone) call?
4 What is the date on the letter? / What date is on the letter? /
On what date was the letter written?

(4 marks)

Test 50

50.1
1 traveller's cheques
2 a ticket
3 currency
4 a package holiday
5 nightlife
6 your luggage
7 a phrase book
8 postcards
9 the Tourist (Information) Office
10 a ferry

(10 marks)

50.2
1 a large comfortable *bus*
2 they look at your *passport*
3 a special *visa*
4 across *the sea*
5 in a *tent*

(5 marks)

50.3
1 had
2 flew
3 ferry
4 by
5 by
6 food
7 nightlife
8 speak
9 phrase book
10 going
11 go
12 tent
13 car
14 traveller's cheques
15 currency

(15 marks)

Test 51

51.1
1 a butcher / a butcher's
2 a toy shop
3 a baker / a baker's
4 a gift shop
5 a supermarket

6 a chemist / a chemist's / a pharmacy
7 a newsagent / a newsagent's
8 a post office
9 a hairdresser / a hairdresser's
10 a book shop   (10 marks)

51.2
1 stationery
2 electrical goods
3 childrenswear /children's clothes / children's clothing
4 ladieswear/womenswear or ladies'/women's clothes/clothing
5 cosmetics
6 sports (equipment)
7 furniture
8 menswear / men's clothes / men's clothing   (8 marks)

51.3
1   CUSTOMER: The *shop assistant* said I could change it as long as I kept the *receipt*.
2   CUSTOMER: Where can I pay for this, please?
    SHOP ASSISTANT: You can pay at that *cash desk / cash register* over there.
                   (*till* or *counter* is also possible)
3   SHOP ASSISTANT: Can I *help* you, madam?
    CUSTOMER: Yes, how much does this hat *cost*?
    SHOP ASSISTANT: Oh, let's see. Here we are – €35.
4   (In a small café)
    CUSTOMER: Can I pay by *credit* card?
    WAITER: Sorry, sir, we don't have a machine.
    CUSTOMER: Oh. Can I write a *cheque*?
    WAITER: No, I'm very sorry, sir, *cash* only. This is just a small café.
5   SALLY: I like this sweater. Shall I buy it?
    MARY: Why don't you *try* it on first and see how it looks on you?
    SALLY: Yes, maybe I should.
6   (The customer has just bought a scarf)
    SHOP ASSISTANT: There you are, madam. $25, and here's your *change*, $5.
                   Shall I put it in a (*carrier*) *bag* for you?
    CUSTOMER: No thanks. I'll put it on. It's cold today!
7   CUSTOMER: I bought this jacket yesterday. It's too big for me.
              Do you have it in a smaller *size*?   (12 marks)

Test 52

52.1
1 key   3 (tele)phone   5 lift   7 bill   9 hair dryer
2 shower   4 luggage   6 form   8 reception   10 kettle   (10 marks)

52.2
1 have   3 sign   5 have   7 cash   9 change
2 fill in   4 Check   6 get   8 book   10 check out   (10 marks)

52.3
1 your bill   5 a double room   9 reception
2 the lift   6 the (country) code (for Britain)   10 a kettle
3 a key   7 a morning call
4 a single room   8 reservation / booking   (10 marks)

Test 53

53.1   1 d   2 e   3 f   4 b   5 a   6 c   (6 marks)

53.2   1 snack   4 list
           2 rare; medium; well-done   5 starters; desserts; vegetarian
           3 soft   6 order   (20 marks)

53.3   1 roast beef   3 mashed potatoes
           2 plain omelette   4 chocolate gateau

   (Note: *roast potatoes* and *plain chocolate* are also possible.)   (4 marks)

Test 54

54.1   1 He is going running.   6 They are going motor racing.
           2 She is going skiing.   7 They are playing cricket.
           3 They are playing baseball.   8 They are playing rugby.
           4 They are playing table tennis.   9 They are playing basketball.
           5 They are going canoeing.   10 She is going swimming.

   (10 marks: ½ for the sport and ½ for the right verb – *go* or *play*)

54.2   1 a swimming pool   6 judo, karate (2 marks)
           2 a football pitch/field   7 horse racing
           3 a basketball court   8 tennis / table tennis / badminton
           4 skiing   9 motor racing
           5 football   (10 marks)

54.3   1 Skiing – because the others are all done on water.
           2 Running – because the others all use other things to help the person go faster (they use a
             boat or a horse or a car). / Sailing – it is on water and the others are all on land.
           3 Badminton – because the others all use balls. / Baseball – because the others all use nets.
           4 Rugby – because the others all use round balls. / Table tennis – because the others are all
             team sports.
           5 American football – because the others are all played on a court. / Tennis – because the
             others are all team sports.

   (10 marks: 1 for the correct sport, 1 for the correct reason)

Test 55

55.1   1 science fiction   6 action
           2 horror   7 crime/detective (2 marks)
           3 western   8 comedy
           4 cartoon   9 love story
           5 musical   (10 marks)

55.2   1 What's on *at* the cinema
           2 relax and *watch* videos
           3 I was *bored* / It was *boring* ('I was boring' means <u>you</u> made other people bored!)
           4 to *the* cinema
           5 I enjoyed *it* very much
           6 film *on* TV   (12 marks)

55.3
1 action
2 cartoon
3 science fiction
4 comedy
5 love story / romantic film / romance
6 horror
7 western (sometimes also called *cowboy films*)
8 detective/crime (sometimes also called *thrillers*) (8 marks)

Test 56

56.1
1 true
2 false – She is playing a computer game.
3 false – He is watching a film on TV.
4 false – She is gardening.
5 true
6 false – He is listening to a CD.

(10 marks: 1 for correctly labelling each sentence true or false;
1 for correcting each of the four false statements)

56.2
1 invite 3 ring 5 grown 7 see/watch 9 stay
2 had   4 cook 6 watch/see 8 talk   10 use   (10 marks)

56.3
1 Grandfather always has a sleep after lunch. / After lunch Grandfather always has a sleep.
2 I like reading books about famous people.
3 I usually listen to the radio in my car.
4 My favourite films are musicals.
5 My mother has a lot of house plants.   (10 marks)

Test 57

57.1
1 murder
2 mug
3 terrorism / terrorist attack
4 car thief
5 steal
6 robbery
7 robber
8 shoplifter
9 burglary
10 pusher/dealer   (10 marks)

57.2
1 burglary; broke; stole/took
2 murdered; murderer
3 Shoplifting; shoplifters
4 robbed; robbers
5 mugged
6 thief; thefts / car thefts   (12 marks)

57.3
1 innocent
2 a fine
3 vandalism; vandals
4 to arrest someone
5 (football) hooliganism
6 a court
7 prison   (8 marks)

Test 58

58.1 [1 c] 2 k 3 e 4 f 5 d 6 a 7 j 8 b 9 g 10 h 11 i   (10 marks)

58.2

```
²W O M E N ¹S M A G A Z I N E
³J O U R N A L I S T
        ⁴I N T E R V I E W
        ⁵R E P O R T E R
      ⁶T A L K S H O W
        L
      ⁷C O M I C
⁸C O M P U T E R
    ⁹I N T E R N E T
        D
        I
      ¹⁰S O A P
    ¹¹C H A N N E L
```

(10 marks)

58.3 newspaper: morning, evening
magazine: women's, computer, teenage   (10 marks: 2 for each)

Test 59

59.1
1 It's broken.   4 It's not working.
2 It's dying.   5 It's untidy.
3 He's cut his finger.   (10 marks)

59.2
1 put a plaster on it
2 2 of the following: repair it / mend it / fix it / throw it away
3 tidy it (up)
4 water it / throw it away   (10 marks: 2 each)

59.3
1 crashed   4 apologise   7 look for
2 mood   5 row   8 untidy; tidy (2 marks)
3 order   6 lost   9 mend/repair/fix   (10 marks)

Test 60

60.1
1 strike   4 snowstorm   7 pollution   10 earthquake
2 traffic jam   5 forest fire   8 car crash
3 hurricane   6 flood   9 unemployment   (10 marks)

60.2
1 Poor   4 polluted   7 flooded   10 War of Independence
2 Unemployed   5 hungry   8 on strike
3 Homeless   6 rush hour   9 catch fire   (10 marks)

60.3
car crash   rush hour
air pollution   traffic jam
earthquake   homeless people
snowstorm   crowded cities
forest fire   strong wind   (10 marks)

Personal diary

Test	Word	Translation	Points to remember	Related words

Personal diary

Test	Word	Translation	Points to remember	Related words

Phonemic symbols

Vowel sounds

Symbol	Examples		
/iː/	sleep	me	
/i/	happy	recipe	
/ɪ/	pin	dinner	
/ʊ/	foot	could	pull
/uː/	do	shoe	through
/e/	red	head	said
/ə/	arrive	father	colour
/ɜː/	turn	bird	work
/ɔː/	sort	thought	walk
/æ/	cat	black	
/ʌ/	sun	enough	wonder
/ɒ/	got	watch	sock
/ɑː/	part	heart	laugh

Symbol	Examples		
/eɪ/	name	late	aim
/aɪ/	my	idea	time
/ɔɪ/	boy	noise	
/eə/	pair	where	bear
/ɪə/	hear	beer	
/əʊ/	go	home	show
/aʊ/	out	cow	
/ʊə/	pure	fewer	

Consonant sounds

Symbol	Examples		
/p/	put		
/b/	book		
/t/	take		
/d/	dog		
/k/	car	kick	
/g/	go	guarantee	
/tʃ/	catch	church	
/dʒ/	age	lounge	
/f/	for	cough	
/v/	love	vehicle	
/θ/	thick	path	
/ð/	this	mother	
/s/	since	rice	
/z/	zoo	houses	
/ʃ/	shop	sugar	machine
/ʒ/	pleasure	usual	vision
/h/	hear	hotel	
/m/	make		
/n/	name	now	
/ŋ/	bring		
/l/	look	while	
/r/	road		
/j/	young		
/w/	wear		

Acknowledgements

We are very grateful to the following teachers who commented on the material:
Lynda Edwards, Dorset, UK
Monica Flood, Milan, Italy
Chris Nicol, Sophia Antipolis, France

We would also like to thank our editors at Cambridge University Press, in particular Nóirín Burke, Rachel Harrison and Julie Moore whose expert advice has been invaluable throughout the production of these tests.

Michael McCarthy
Felicity O'Dell
Cambridge, September 2003